DETROIT PUBLIC LIBRARY

P9-CCZ-030

CHASE BRANCH LIBRARY
17731 W. SEVEN MILE
DETROIT. MICH. 48235

APR 3 0 2001

ch

PAUL LAURENCE DUNBAR

The **African-American Biographies** Series

MARIAN ANDERSON
Singer and Humanitarian
0-7660-1211-5

MAYA ANGELOU
More Than a Poet
0-89490-684-4

LOUIS ARMSTRONG
King of Jazz
0-89490-997-5

ARTHUR ASHE
Breaking the Color Barrier
in Tennis
0-89490-689-5

BENJAMIN BANNEKER
Astronomer and Mathematician
0-7660-1208-5

RALPH BUNCHE
Winner of the Nobel Peace Prize
0-7660-1203-4

W. E. B. DU BOIS
Champion of Civil Rights
0-7660-1209-3

PAUL LAURENCE DUNBAR
Portrait of a Poet
0-7660-1350-2

DUKE ELLINGTON
Giant of Jazz
0-89490-691-7

ARETHA FRANKLIN
Motown Superstar
0-89490-686-0

NIKKI GIOVANNI
Poet of the People
0-7660-1238-7

WHOOPI GOLDBERG
Comedian and Movie Star
0-7660-1205-0

LORRAINE HANSBERRY
Playwright and Voice of Justice
0-89490-945-2

LANGSTON HUGHES
Poet of the
Harlem Renaissance
0-89490-815-4

ZORA NEALE HURSTON
Southern Storyteller
0-89490-685-2

JESSE JACKSON
Civil Rights Activist
0-7660-1390-1

QUINCY JONES
Musician, Composer, Producer
0-89490-814-6

BARBARA JORDAN
Congresswoman, Lawyer,
Educator
0-89490-692-5

CORETTA SCOTT KING
Striving for Civil Rights
0-89490-811-1

MARTIN LUTHER KING, JR.
Leader for Civil Rights
0-89490-687-9

TONI MORRISON
Nobel Prize-Winning Author
0-89490-688-7

WALTER DEAN MYERS
Writer for Real Teens
0-7660-1206-9

JESSE OWENS
Track and Field Legend
0-89490-812-X

COLIN POWELL
Soldier and Patriot
0-89490-810-3

PAUL ROBESON
Actor, Singer,
Political Activist
0-89490-944-4

JACKIE ROBINSON
Baseball's Civil Rights Legend
0-89490-690-9

BETTY SHABAZZ
Sharing the Vision of Malcolm X
0-7660-1210-7

MADAM C. J. WALKER
Self-Made Businesswoman
0-7660-1204-2

IDA B. WELLS-BARNETT
Crusader Against Lynching
0-89490-947-9

OPRAH WINFREY
Talk Show Legend
0-7660-1207-7

CARTER G. WOODSON
Father of African-American History
0-89490-946-0

—African-American Biographies—

PAUL LAURENCE DUNBAR

Portrait of a Poet

Series Consultant:
Dr. Russell L. Adams, Chairman
Department of Afro-American Studies, Howard University

Catherine Reef

 Enslow Publishers, Inc.

40 Industrial Road	PO Box 38
Box 398	Aldershot
Berkeley Heights, NJ 07922	Hants GU12 6BP
USA	UK

http://www.enslow.com

Copyright © 2000 by Catherine Reef

All rights reserved.

No part of this book may be reproduced by any means
without the written permission of the publisher.

Library of Congress Cataloging-in-Publication Data

Reef, Catherine.
    Paul Laurence Dunbar : portrait of a poet / Catherine Reef.
        p. cm. — (African-American biographies)
    "Works by Paul Laurence Dunbar": p.
    Includes bibliographical references (p.   ) and index.
    Summary: A biography of the poet who faced racism and devoted
himself to depicting the black experience in America.
    ISBN 0-7660-1350-2
    1. Dunbar, Paul Laurence, 1872–1906 Juvenile literature. 2. Poets,
American—19th century Biography Juvenile literature. 3. Afro-American
poets Biography Juvenile literature. 4. Afro-Americans in literature
Juvenile literature. [1. Dunbar, Paul Laurence, 1872–1906. 2. Poets,
American. 3. Afro-Americans Biography.] I. Title. II. Series.
PS1557.R34   2000
811'.4—dc21
[B]
                                                    99-16456
                                                        CIP

Printed in the United States of America

10 9 8 7 6 5 4 3 2 1

To Our Readers: All Internet addresses in this book were active and appropriate
when we went to press. Any comments or suggestions can be sent by e-mail to
Comments@enslow.com or to the address on the back cover.

Illustration Credits: Chicago Historical Society, photograph ICHi-
02525, C. D. Arnold, photographer, p. 38; Courtesy, American
Antiquarian Society, p. 81; From the collections of the Montgomery
County Historical Society, Dayton, Ohio, p. 28; Historical Society of
Washington, D.C., p. 62; Library of Congress, pp. 9, 29, 43, 47, 51, 59,
70, 74, 89, 94, 96, 107; Ohio Historical Society, pp. 101, 108;
Photographs and Prints Division, Schomburg Center for Research in
Black Culture, The New York Public Library, Astor, Lenox, and Tilden
Foundations, pp. 14, 20, 57, 77.

Cover Illustration: National Portrait Gallery, Smithsonian Institution
Oil on canvas by William McKnight Farrow

CONTENTS

1 A Worthy Singer 7

2 Being a Boy 15

3 Dreaming All the Time 25

4 Fame's Bright Sky 35

5 Pen and Voice 49

6 The Caged Bird 61

7 An Unknown Country 73

8 No Rest 85

9 Back Home 93

10 Singing to the Dawn 103

Chronology 110

Works by Paul Laurence
    Dunbar 113

Chapter Notes 115

Further Reading with
    Internet Addresses 124

Index 126

1

A WORTHY
SINGER

he man at the door had a wrinkled face and a body bent from years of hard labor. His worn clothing made him look out of place in this stylish neighborhood of Washington, D.C. For much of his life, the old man had worked as a slave on an Alabama plantation. It was now 1898, and he had been a free citizen for thirty-three years. But he never would forget his years of enslavement.

Paul Laurence Dunbar invited the man in, asked him to sit down, and offered him something to drink. Dunbar's gentle manners made the man feel right at home. Dunbar appeared to have little in common with his guest. Dunbar was in his mid-twenties, expensively dressed, slim, and agile. He was also famous. In the closing years of the nineteenth century, he was one of America's best-known writers. He was the first African American to earn his living writing poetry, novels, magazine articles, and essays.

Dunbar's own parents had been born into slavery, though. He felt a kinship with people like this man, the former slaves who lived in Howard Town, a poor section of the city. He liked to listen as they talked about the past, even though they might bring up painful memories of life before the Civil War.[1] Dunbar was writing a collection of stories titled *Folks from Dixie* based on their recollections.

On this day, the visitor told a disturbing tale about something that happened after slavery had ended. He told about the lynching of his nephew, a young man wrongly accused of a crime. "Night riders"—local whites acting under cover of darkness—had snatched the youth from his jail cell and carried him off. Denying him a trial, they had hanged him from a mammoth oak tree. From that time forward, while most of the tree flourished, the branch from which his nephew had hung dried up and died. People whispered that the nephew's ghost haunted the tree, the old man said.

The story touched Dunbar deeply.[2] He knew that too many African Americans had suffered injustice and

Paul Laurence Dunbar

death at the hands of white mobs. Lynchings like the one the old man described were far too common in the United States of America. In one recent year, 1892, more than 160 African Americans had been executed by their fellow citizens.

As soon as the old man finished talking, Dunbar went to his desk. A poem was taking shape in his imagination, and he wanted to get it on paper. He wrote:

> *Pray why are you so bare, so bare,*
> *Oh, bough of the old oak-tree;*
> *And why when I go through the shade you throw,*
> *Runs a shudder over me?*[3]

Dunbar wrote more stanzas in which the oak tree describes the lynching. The tree cannot forget the death of the innocent victim. In Dunbar's version of the tale, a tormenting memory, and not a ghost, haunts the oak:

> *I feel the rope against my bark,*
> *And the weight of him in my grain,*
> *I feel in the throe of his final woe*
> *The touch of my own last pain.*[4]

Many poets spend hours searching for the precise words to convey their thoughts and feelings. Dunbar was luckier than most, because words and phrases came to his mind easily. A friend of his once joked that Dunbar should hang up a sign that read, "Poems while you wait."[5] The friend later explained that to be able to think and write at the same time is a rare gift, and "Paul Dunbar had this gift."[6]

Dunbar wrote more than one hundred poems like "The Haunted Oak," poems drawn from African-American experience. His poems could be serious or sad, joyful or humorous. He celebrated the beauty of women with black skin and described the delight of an African-American father bouncing a child on his knee. "Every phase of Negro life has been caught by his pen as by a camera," said W. S. Scarborough, an African-American scholar, in 1914.[7]

African Americans memorized Dunbar's verses and recited them at social gatherings. "You didn't say a Dunbar poem—you *performed* it," said the writer Arna Bontemps, recalling those pleasant occasions.[8] Dunbar's poetry was meant to be read aloud, so African-American parents read it to their children. Proud of this great writer, they hung Dunbar's portrait in their dining rooms and parlors.

White fans flocked to the many readings that Dunbar gave throughout the country. He was a popular entertainer. He was full of energy on stage and often acted out his poems. No one else could bring Dunbar's words to life as well as the poet himself could. "His voice was a perfect instrument and he knew how to use it," said the writer James Weldon Johnson, who was Dunbar's friend.[9]

Dunbar was also a social critic at a time when few

people spoke out about race relations. He wrote poems, stories, and newspaper articles that expressed his outrage at discrimination in northern cities, at unequal treatment of black and white soldiers, and, of course, at lynchings. He made people think—and perhaps think twice—about racial problems.

Dunbar has been a role model for the African-American writers who came after him. Langston Hughes, who published his first book of poems in the 1920s, was inspired to write some of his poems after reading Dunbar's work. Gwendolyn Brooks, who won the Pulitzer Prize in poetry in 1950, dreamed of being the female Paul Laurence Dunbar while she was growing up.[10] And Dunbar continues to influence writers. Maya Angelou selected a line from the poem "Sympathy" as the title of her 1970 autobiography, *I Know Why the Caged Bird Sings*. By doing so, she declared herself one of Dunbar's literary descendants. "Paul Laurence Dunbar is a natural resource of our people," said the contemporary poet Nikki Giovanni.[11]

As a beginning poet, Dunbar longed, he said, "to be a worthy singer of the songs of God and of nature. To be able to interpret my own people through song and story, and to prove to the many that after all we are more human than African."[12] His goal was simple and at the same time staggering: to show, in his writing, that people of all races are more alike than they are different. Dunbar wrote at a time when many whites viewed Africa as an uncivilized place, and Africans as inferior. He bore witness to the fact that African Americans feel the same emotions that people of European descent do. The human feeling that shines through his poetry has made Paul Laurence Dunbar one of America's best-loved authors.

Matilda Dunbar, the poet's mother, lived through difficult times,
but she preferred to look on the bright side of life.

2

BEING A BOY

Paul Laurence Dunbar grew up hearing stories and songs. As a boy in Dayton, Ohio, he often listened to his mother talk about slavery. Matilda Dunbar had spent the first twenty years of her life as an enslaved household worker in Kentucky. Now a free woman, she took in laundry from Dayton's hotels. As she scrubbed stains out of tablecloths and ironed linen napkins, she told Paul about the past.

Matilda Dunbar looked on the bright side of life. She focused on happy memories, such as parties in the slave quarters and kindnesses received. She kept the dark side of slavery—the whippings, the splitting up of families, the denial of basic freedom—to herself. Paul listened carefully. His mother's stories, and the hymns and spirituals that she sang, would later inspire some of his finest poems.

Paul's father, Joshua Dunbar, told stories, too. He remained bitter about his treatment under slavery and used harsh words to describe his experiences. Paul's father also talked often about the Civil War. He had fought with the 55th Massachusetts Volunteer Infantry, a unit of African-American soldiers led by white officers. He was one of the 186,000 African Americans who fought for the Union—the Northern side in the war. African-American soldiers took part in more than four hundred Civil War battles. The 55th Infantry saw action in the swamps of Florida and on the coastal islands of South Carolina.

Joshua Dunbar plastered walls for a living, practicing a trade he had learned when he was a slave in Kentucky. He had run away from his owner in the mid-nineteenth century and traveled north on the Underground Railroad. This was a secret network of people who sheltered African Americans fleeing slavery. Both Dayton and the city of Cincinnati, Ohio, fifty miles to the south, had been busy stops on the Underground Railroad. Their citizens had been active opponents of slavery.

The Underground Railroad took Joshua Dunbar all the way to Canada. There, he was safe from the slave catchers who prowled northern cities and who might whisk him back to the South and slavery. Paul's father left the security of Canada in 1861, when the Civil War broke out, so that he could fight to free his race. When the war ended, he made his way to Dayton, where he met Matilda Murphy, a young widow with two sons, Robert and William, called Rob and Buddy. Joshua and Matilda were married in 1871, and Paul was born on June 27, 1872. A daughter was born the following year, but she died at the age of two. Like most former slaves and their children in the North, the Dunbar family lived simply and plainly.

But they did not live peacefully. Paul often heard his parents arguing when he was small. More than once, he saw his father storm out of the house, slamming the door behind him. The Dunbars' marriage was an unhappy one, and Paul's father soon moved into the Old Soldiers' Home, which was not far from the house where his wife and the children lived. Joshua and Matilda Dunbar divorced in 1876.

Paul never felt close to stern Joshua Dunbar, who gave orders to his family as if they were soldiers in a regiment.[1] He was proud of his father's achievements, though. One of his first poems, "Emancipation," was a tribute to Joshua Dunbar's love of freedom:

Never again shall the manacles gall you
Never again shall the whip stroke defame!
Nobles and Freemen, your destinies call you
Onward to honor, to glory and fame.[2]

Honor, glory, and fame. Matilda Dunbar was sure that Paul would attain all of those things. He learned so quickly and had such a way with words. Like most slaves, Paul's mother had never learned to read and write. Now she attended night classes so that she could help him study. She vowed to work hard and sacrifice to give him a good education.

Paul was a quiet, serious boy who read many books and received good grades. In the summer, when school was out, he dangled his feet in Dayton's rivers, the Miami and the Stillwater, waiting to hook a fish. He listened to the songs of birds in the branches over his head. On hot days, he and his friends stripped off their clothes and swam in the cool river water. Dunbar remembered those carefree times in the poem "A Boy's Summer Song," in which he asked, "On a summer's day, / What's so fine as being a boy?"[3]

For Paul, being a boy also meant helping to support his mother. Joshua Dunbar provided for his son until his death, which occurred when Paul was twelve. At that time, Rob and Buddy were young men starting families of their own. They had little money to spare for their mother. Paul raked leaves, cut grass, and did other odd jobs to earn a little cash.

Dayton was a city of thirty thousand people when Paul Dunbar was born. This prosperous trading center was situated at the heart of a rich agricultural region. Several streams flowed through the city, and they often overran their banks in the spring. The number of African Americans in Dayton at the time is unknown, but the black community played an active role in city life. There were African-American grocers, blacksmiths, and restaurant owners. The African-American churches sponsored social activities for their congregations.

Church members also got together to discuss the ideas of African-American leaders such as Alexander Crummell and Frederick Douglass. Crummell (1819–1898) was a scholar and missionary who worked to improve life for black people throughout the world. He popularized the concept of pan-Africanism, which is a belief in the unity of all people of African descent. Crummell liked to say, "A race is a family."[4] Douglass (1817–1895), who had escaped from slavery in 1838, had gained fame as an antislavery speaker and writer. After the Civil War, he continued to speak out about the unequal treatment of African Americans.

The growing city of Dayton, with a population that would pass sixty-one thousand in 1890, had just one high school. Most young Americans in the late nineteenth century, whether black or white, dropped out of school by the end of the eighth grade. They either went to work or helped out at home or on their family farm. Only good students whose families could do without their assistance attended Central High School. The Dunbars would have had fewer financial worries if

Paul had found a full-time job. But Matilda Dunbar was determined to see him graduate from high school.

Nearly everyone enrolled at Central High School was white. Paul was the only African American in his class, but he never felt singled out because of his race. He was a popular student whose talent with words served him well. He was on the debating team, he edited the school newspaper, and he was president of the Philomathean Society, the high school literary club. Mrs. Truesdale, Mr. Wilson, and the other teachers

Dunbar, top left, with the other members of the Philomathean Society, his high school literary club.

praised the poems that he wrote and urged him to write more.

Paul needed little encouragement. He had been steadily submitting poems to local newspapers, only to have them returned. Then, in 1888, the *Dayton Herald* printed three of his poems. One, "Our Martyred Soldiers," honored the men who died in the Civil War. The poem displayed a knowledge of life's hardships that most readers would expect from a writer much older than sixteen. For example, Dunbar understood that, in death, the soldiers had found greater peace than many of the living enjoyed. He wrote:

> *Beneath the dew, the rain, the snow,*
> *They heed no more the bloody foe,*
> *Their sleep is calm, to them alone*
> *'Tis giv'n to lie without a moan.*[5]

Paul Dunbar wrote plays as well as poetry. When he formed a school drama troupe, many students asked to join. Some offered to sing or play musical instruments, while others wanted to act. The group rehearsed at the Dunbar home and performed in churches and at public events.

Paul's friends were both black and white. One of his best pals, Robert Burns, was an African American who was a year older than Paul. After graduating from high school, Bud Burns went away to college to fulfill his dream of becoming a doctor. Another good friend was a white classmate, Orville Wright, who would drop out before graduating. In 1903, Orville and his brother, Wilbur, would become famous for inventing the first successful powered airplane. As teenagers, the Wrights already loved to tinker. They owned a printing press, and together with Dunbar published a weekly newspaper, the *West Side News*.

In 1890, when he was eighteen, Paul told Orville Wright that he had an idea. He wanted to start a newspaper of his own for the African Americans of Dayton. Orville liked his friend's plan. Knowing from experience that it would take time for Paul to get enough subscribers to pay the paper's expenses, Orville offered to print the first few issues free of charge.

The newspaper was to benefit African Americans in several ways. It would encourage those who wanted to open businesses or begin civic projects. It would give a voice to young people by printing their articles and poems. And it would inform people about politics. Paul made it clear that his newspaper would also be a forum for the discussion of race. It was not enough, he said, for people to put their thoughts about racism into words. They needed to take action in order to create change. "The time has come when you should act your opinions out," he told his readers. "For your own sake, for the sake of Heaven and the race, stop saying, and go to doing."[6]

During Dunbar's lifetime, most African Americans lived in the South. Their lives had changed little since the abolition of slavery. They worked for low wages, growing cotton, tobacco, and the other crops they had raised while enslaved. Beginning in 1866, the southern states had enacted "Black Codes," which were laws that restricted the activity of African Americans. For example, Mississippi's Black Code barred African Americans from owning land, preaching, or possessing firearms. It was against the law in Louisiana for African Americans to leave their workplace without permission. White supremacist groups such as the Ku Klux Klan operated outside the law to terrorize the black population.

Life was better for African Americans in the North, but there were many neighborhoods where they could not buy or rent a home. Northern blacks earned less money than whites did, and they had fewer career and educational opportunities.

Paul went from door to door, urging the African Americans of Dayton to subscribe to his weekly paper, *The Tattler*. "Young men save a dollar and a half from pleasure and help support a colored journal," he pleaded in the first issue.[7] But too few people had $1.50 to spare, and *The Tattler* ceased publication after the eighth issue was printed.

Paul Dunbar may have failed as a newspaperman, but he continued to touch people with his poetry. As graduation neared, his friends and teachers asked him to write lyrics for their class song. On a June night in

1891, the forty-three graduating seniors of Central High School stood before their proud families in Dayton's Grand Opera House. They sang a song that expressed their readiness to move forward in life. In his lyrics, Paul had compared the graduating students to sailors embarking on a voyage. The students sang:

> *And now, the world we fear no more,*
> *As here we stand upon the shore,*
> *Prepared to cast our moorings free,*
> *And breast the waves of future's sea.*[8]

3

DREAMING ALL
THE TIME

he new high school graduates took their places in the adult world. Paul Dunbar was nineteen, and it was time for him to choose a career.

His mother urged him to become a minister. In her mind, she could see him wearing a clergyman's collar and preaching on Sunday mornings. As a minister, he could use his education to enlighten others. She could think of no finer profession for him to enter.

Her son felt no religious calling, though. Instead, he sometimes saw himself as a journalist who was on the scene when news was happening. He imagined writing articles for the front page of the newspaper, bringing current events to life. At other times, he thought about being a lawyer and arguing cases in court.

Dunbar knew that, for him, a career in law was only a dream. His family had no money to pay for college. And it looked as though he would never be a reporter either. The editor of the *Dayton Herald* said flat out that he would not hire an African American to write the news.

Still, Dunbar was optimistic. In 1891, a high school diploma and good grades were enough to get a young person hired in a bank or an office. Dunbar went all over Dayton, from one place of business to another, applying for jobs. He was willing to work hard and learn, but everywhere he was told the same thing: African Americans need not apply.

Dunbar remembered this experience when he wrote the short story "One Man's Fortunes," published in 1903. In the story, an African American named Bert Halliday graduates from college and looks for a job in the midwestern city where he grew up. He is shocked to discover that the only positions open to him are waiter or janitor. For a while he is hired to work in the office of a white lawyer, but only because the lawyer is running for office and wants the black vote. When the lawyer achieves that goal, he fires Halliday. A bitter Halliday concludes, "I now see why so many promising

young men, class orators, valedictorians and the like
fall by the wayside and are never heard from after commencement day. . . . They get tired of swimming
against the tide, as who would not?"[1]

Dunbar, too, got tired of swimming against the
tide. After a summer of searching, he took the only job
he could find, as an elevator operator in the Callahan
Building, a downtown office structure. For eleven
hours a day, he carried passengers to the upper floors
of the building and back down again. His employer
had no use for his learning or literary talent and paid
him $4 a week. That was a small salary, but money
stretched further in 1891 than it does today. A shopper
could buy a bar of soap for 5 cents and a can of soup
for 8 cents. A pair of sturdy work shoes cost $1, the
same as a visit to the dentist. Those $4 helped Dunbar
and his mother pay their expenses.

The new job was a letdown, but Dunbar used his
time as well as he could. When there were no passengers in his elevator, he pulled out a book of poems. He
read all kinds of poetry, but he liked the nineteenth-
century English poets best, especially Alfred, Lord
Tennyson. Tennyson (1809–1892) is remembered for
such works as *Idylls of the King*, a retelling of the King
Arthur legend in verse.

Dunbar also read poems by American writers who
were popular in his day. He lived at a time when
many people read poetry for entertainment. Monthly

"So many promising young men . . . get tired of swimming against the tide": Despite his education, Dunbar, as an African American, had to settle for a job as an elevator operator. He worked in the Callahan Building—center, with the tower—in downtown Dayton, Ohio.

magazines such as *Century* printed new poems by Eugene Field, James Whitcomb Riley, and other authors. Field (1850–1895) is known best for his children's poems, including "Wynken, Blynken, and Nod" about a child falling asleep. Riley (1849–1916) was one of Dunbar's favorites. Known as the "Hoosier poet," Riley found inspiration among the people of his home state, Indiana, and took a fond look at country life. He wrote many of his poems in the dialect of his region, spelling words the way native midwesterners pronounced them. One of his best-loved poems was "The Old Swimmin'-Hole":

> *Oh! the old swimmin'-hole! Whare the crick so still*
> *and deep*
> *Looked like a baby-river that was laying half asleep,*
> *And the gurgle of the worter round the drift jest below*
> *Sounded like the laugh of something we onc't ust to*
> *know . . .* [2]

Americans were reading other kinds of poetry as well. Poems in the "plantation tradition" painted a rosy

One of Dunbar's favorite poets was the popular James Whitcomb Riley, above, surrounded by young friends.

picture of slave life in the South. These poems, written by white authors, showed slavery as many whites wished it had been, and not as it really was. The authors presented the years of slavery as a happy time and portrayed slaves who were content with their lowly status. The slaves loved their masters, who were always kind. Often, the poems featured former slaves looking back on their lives before the Civil War and regretting that slavery had ended.

The best-known poet of the plantation tradition was Irwin Russell (1853–1879), a Mississippi native. In one of Russell's poems, "Mahsr [Master] John," a newly freed African American pities his old master, who lost his slaves and property after the war. The speaker in the poem declares:

> *He had to pay his debts, an' so his lan' is mos'ly*
> *gone—*
> *An' I declar I's sorry fur my pore ol' Mahsr John.*[3]

Poets such as Irwin Russell claimed to write in dialect, but they never bothered with accuracy. Rather than capturing the actual speech of African Americans, they carelessly filled their lines with errors in grammar and pronunciation. Their work appeared in national magazines, and readers in both the South and the North enjoyed it. But these poems promoted the idea that African Americans were simpleminded. They encouraged racial prejudice.

Plantation poetry, new American poems, old

English legends—Paul Dunbar studied them all. When Dunbar read a poem, he did more than savor the beauty of its rhymes and rhythms. Like Orville Wright fiddling with a piece of machinery, Dunbar examined each part of the poem separately. He took the lines apart and looked at every word until he figured out how the author had used them all to create the finished work. He applied the lessons he learned to his own verses. He began to nurture a dream of being a professional writer.

People's accents fascinated Dunbar. He listened to conversations in the elevator he operated, and he tried to guess where the riders came from. While he wrote many poems in the formal English of Tennyson, he wrote others in dialect. Dunbar had a keen memory for the way people pronounced words, and he captured the sounds of everyday speech in his writing. "The Ol' Tunes" is one of Dunbar's early poems written in the midwestern dialect favored by James Whitcomb Riley:

> *You kin talk about yer anthems*
> *An' yer arias an' sich,*
> *An' yer modern choir-singin'*
> *That you think so awful rich;*
> *But you orter heerd us youngsters*
> *In the times now far away,*
> *A-singin' o' the ol' tunes*
> *In the ol'-fashioned way.*[4]

A few of his poems and stories appeared in magazines, and in December 1891, he received his first payment for a written piece. The Kellogg Newspaper Company of Chicago paid him $6 for a story set on the western frontier. Still, Dunbar felt discouraged. Earning a living as a writer seemed impossibly hard. And his regular job took up time that he would have liked to spend on his poems. He jotted in a notebook:

What's the use of dreaming all the time
Yes there's lots of hope a-beaming through your rhyme
But the work you've got to do
Dreams won't ever do for you
Even if they did come true.[5]

Then, in the early summer of 1892, it looked as though dreams might start coming true for Paul Dunbar. He opened the door of his elevator one day to see Mrs. Truesdale, his teacher from Central High School, standing in the lobby of the Callahan Building. Truesdale was surprised to run into her old student and glad to learn that he was still writing. She said that the Western Association of Writers was holding its convention in Dayton during the last week of June. She asked Dunbar if he would like to read some of his poetry to the group.

Dunbar jumped at the chance. On his twentieth birthday, June 27, 1892, he took time off from work to go to the Grand Opera House, where the western writers had gathered. It was a hot morning. The women in the audience fanned themselves as the presiding officer stepped forward to introduce the poet Paul Dunbar.

James Newton Matthews, a writer from Mason, Illinois, described what happened next: "Great was the surprise of the audience to see stepping lightly down the aisle between the rows of fluttering fans and the assembled beauty and wit of Dayton, a slender Negro lad."[6] Dunbar looked calm and professional as he stepped up to the podium. He recited a poem he had written especially for the occasion, offering the writers "A welcome warm as Western wine, / and free as Western hearts . . ."[7]

Matthews applauded as heartily as everyone else did when Dunbar finished his reading. Dunbar "then disappeared from the hall as suddenly as he had entered it," Matthews wrote.[8] Dunbar could not stay to shake any hands because he was expected back at work.

Matthews knew that if he wanted to meet this promising poet, he would have to seek him out. The next morning, he paid a visit to the Callahan Building. He found Dunbar taking a short break, reading the July issue of *Century* magazine and making notes on a pad. Dunbar's break was just about over, so Matthews went with him to the elevator. As they rode up and down, Matthews questioned Dunbar about his life and his writing. Dunbar told him how hard it was to work full-time and write.

Two months later, Dunbar mailed Matthews some poems and a letter. "My hopes are no brighter than when you saw me," Dunbar lamented. He said that he was more disheartened than ever.[9]

Matthews was moved to write an article about the African-American poet for his local newspaper. "Poor Dunbar! He deserves a better fate," Matthews told his readers. "With all his natural brilliancy and capability for better things, he is chained like a galley slave to the ropes of a dingy elevator at starvation wages."[10] Matthews quoted from Dunbar's poems, including "The Ol' Tunes," and he stated, "Show me a white boy of 19 who can excell, or even equal, lines like these."[11]

Not only did Matthews's article bring Dunbar to the public's attention, but it was reprinted in newspapers all over the country. Dunbar received fan mail from people living as far away as Valley Falls, Rhode Island. A man in Montreal, Canada, sent him $20 to buy books. The letter that Dunbar treasured most, though, came from the Indiana poet James Whitcomb Riley. Riley had read about Dunbar in a Denver, Colorado, newspaper and had written to praise his poems. "See how your name is traveling, my chirping friend," Riley said. "And it is a good, sound name, too, that seems to imply the brave, fine spirit of a singer who should command wide and serious attention."[12]

The encouragement from Matthews and Riley fueled a new dream for Dunbar. He dreamed of publishing his poems in a book.

4

FAME'S BRIGHT SKY

or once, Paul Dunbar's dream came true
easily. In early December 1892, he held a
slim volume of poetry in his hands. The
United Brethren Publishing House, a small Dayton
printing company, had published a book of his poems.

Dunbar's first collection of poetry was called *Oak
and Ivy*. He dedicated it to his mother, "To her who has
ever been my guide, teacher and inspiration. . . ."[1] The
book contained fifty-six poems. The first, "Ode to
Ethiopia," was a tribute to Dunbar's race. In the poem,
Ethiopia, a nation in northeast Africa, stands for all
people of African descent. Proud of his race, Dunbar

imagines Ethiopia's name inscribed on a great scroll, flying "High 'mid the clouds of Fame's bright sky."[2]

There were poems that praised beauty and nature in the book, and poems written in dialect. One, "A Banjo Song," was written in the English that Dunbar heard spoken by African Americans from the South:

> *When de quiet, restful shadders*
> *Is beginnin' jes' to fall,—*
> *Den I take de little banjo*
> *F'om its place upon de wall.*[3]

The speech of many African Americans was uniquely suited to dialect writing. The Africans who came to the English colonies and, later, to the United States as slaves had learned English by hearing it. Very few of them ever learned to read or write. Their spoken English evolved from their interpretation of the sounds that they heard and from the lingering influence of African tongues. The speech of their descendants retained a music all its own.

To have *Oak and Ivy* published, Dunbar had agreed to pay the printing costs from the money earned selling the books. If he sold them for a dollar apiece, he would need to sell 125 books to pay the debt. He made some sales to the people who worked in the Callahan Building, and the *High School Times*, Central High School's newspaper, advertised the book. Some members of the Western Association of Writers recommended *Oak and Ivy* to their readers. Within two weeks,

Dunbar sold enough books to repay the publisher. He had earned a profit by Christmas.

As the summer of 1893 approached, Dunbar packed up some copies of *Oak and Ivy*, left his job, and headed for Chicago, Illinois. Chicago was hosting the World's Columbian Exposition, the greatest world's fair of its time. Americans called the exposition "The White City." No one had seen anything like its gleaming marble buildings and shimmering waterways. The fair's sixty-five thousand exhibits celebrated progress in art, science, and industry. Alexander Graham Bell's telephone was on display, and so were the typewriter, the refrigerated railroad car, and other recent inventions. Visitors crowded around the giant Corliss steam engine that stood on a platform fifty-six feet in diameter. There was also a midway where people could watch trained animal acts, eat ostrich-egg omelets, or ride a Ferris wheel 264 feet into the air.

Dunbar was among the thousands of young people who flocked to Chicago to find a job and tour the exposition. He took whatever work he could find, laboring as a waiter, a janitor, and a washroom attendant, and sent most of his earnings to his mother. In his spare time, he marveled at the eleven-ton cheese from Canada, the fifteen-hundred-pound chocolate statue from New York, and the other popular attractions at the fair.

One of the most thrilling moments of Dunbar's trip

Visitors to the World's Columbian Exposition in Chicago in 1893 were dazzled by the architecture and shimmering waterways. Featured in the fair's sixty-five thousand exhibits were the telephone, the typewriter, and other recent inventions.

occurred in June, when he met the famous antislavery activist Frederick Douglass. Douglass, who was nearing the end of his life, had been U.S. minister to Haiti from 1889 until 1891. He had come to the world's fair to serve as commissioner of the Haitian exhibition.

Dunbar described the meeting in a letter to his mother. He wrote, "The old man was just finishing dinner; he got up and came tottering into the room, 'and this is Paul Dunbar,' he said shaking hands and patting me on the shoulder. 'Paul, how do you do? I've been knowing you for some time and you're one of my boys.'"[4] Douglass, who had read about the struggling African-American poet in a newspaper, asked to hear one of his poems. Dunbar recited "Ode to Ethiopia." Then Douglass paged through the copy of *Oak and Ivy* that Dunbar was carrying and chose "The Ol' Tunes" to read aloud. "He seemed delighted," Dunbar proudly told his mother.[5]

Frederick Douglass hired Dunbar as a clerk in the Haitian Building at the exposition and paid him $5 a week. He introduced Dunbar to some of the other bright, talented young African Americans who had come to Chicago that summer. Dunbar met James David Carothers and James Edwin Campbell, who were budding writers like himself. Will Marion Cook was a classically trained violinist and composer who became his friend. Two new female acquaintances, Mary Church Terrell and Ida B. Wells, would later distinguish themselves in the field of civil rights. Dunbar's closest friend that summer was a student from Atlanta University, James Weldon Johnson, who was working at the exposition as a "chair boy." Johnson was one of a thousand young men, white and black, who pushed footsore people through the exhibits in wheelchairs.

Dunbar and his friends had more than one reason for calling the 1893 Chicago exposition the "white city." Many African Americans were complaining about being left out of the world's fair. In Chicago, a city with a large and growing African-American population, no African Americans had been asked to help plan the exhibits. And the president of the Board of Lady Managers, a white society woman named Mrs. Potter Palmer, had refused to work with any black women's groups. The only blacks taking part in the fair were those representing Haiti, a largely black foreign nation that was formerly a French colony, and the one hundred Africans who were performing traditional music and dance in the Dahomey Village, a recreated African settlement.

African Americans agreed that their unique contributions to American culture deserved a place at the fair, but they disagreed about what that place should be. Some people favored a separate building devoted to African-American achievements. Others opposed such a plan, arguing that African Americans already lived too much apart from mainstream American life. A separate building reminded them of the Jim Crow laws that were spreading through the South. Those laws called for segregation of the races in businesses and public places—in railroad cars, waiting rooms, schools, restaurants, theaters, and elsewhere.

At last, hoping to stop the controversy, fair officials decided to host a "Colored People's Day." It was to be a day for displaying the talents of young African Americans, and people of all races were welcome to attend.

Summer was nearly over by the time Colored People's Day, August 25, arrived, but the exposition was as crowded as ever. More than two thousand people filed into Festival Hall, a large auditorium on the fairgrounds. Dunbar waited eagerly with the rest of the audience to hear Frederick Douglass's talk, "The Race Problem in America."

Douglass had barely begun his speech when some white troublemakers in the back of the hall started to shout insults. He tried to proceed, but the jeering made it impossible. So Douglass put aside his prepared remarks and spoke from the heart. In the powerful voice that had once rung out against slavery, he shamed his critics into silence. "Men talk of the Negro problem. There is no Negro problem," Douglass thundered. "The problem is whether the American people have loyalty enough, honor enough, patriotism enough, to live up to their own Constitution."[6] Douglass reminded those present that African Americans had fought for their country in the Civil War. He said that white men from the South, former Confederate soldiers, enjoyed better opportunities in the United States than African Americans did. On behalf of his race, Douglass asked to be treated as well as the whites who had fought against the Union side in the war. He then finished his prepared speech without interruption.

The audience applauded, and Will Marion Cook took the stage, together with Douglass's grandson Joseph. The two played a violin duet that Cook had composed. Next on the program was Paul Dunbar. The poem he recited, "The Colored Soldiers," underscored Douglass's message of patriotism and sacrifice:

> *Yes, the Blacks enjoy their freedom,*
> *And they won it dearly, too;*
> *For the life blood of their thousands*
> *Did the southern fields bedew.*[7]

Dunbar pricked his white listeners' consciences when he noted,

> *They were comrades then and brothers,*
> *Are they more or less to-day?*
> *They were good to stop a bullet*
> *And to front the fearful fray.*
> *They were citizens and soldiers,*
> *When rebellion raised its head;*
> *And the traits that made them worthy,—*
> *Ah! those virtues are not dead.*[8]

Dunbar was thrilled to meet the famous antislavery activist Frederick Douglass, right. Douglass's grandson, Joseph, was an accomplished violinist. Look closely to see a tiny violin on Joseph's tie.

The young people went their separate ways when the exposition closed in October. Paul Dunbar gave journalism another try. He worked briefly for the *Chicago Record* and for some Ohio newspapers. In 1895, he took a temporary job editing the *Indianapolis World*, a newspaper that ran stories of interest to African Americans. He wrote poetry whenever he found the time for it. He wrote one poem in memory of Frederick Douglass, who had recently died.

In the long poem, "Frederick Douglass," he portrayed Ethiopia, or the descendants of Africa, as a woman mourning the loss of a son:

> *She weeps for him a mother's burning tears—*
> *She loved him with a mother's deepest love.*[9]

Dunbar praised Douglass for exposing the evils of slavery:

> *The sunlight of his truth dispelled the mist,*
> *And set in bold relief each dark hued cloud;*
> *To sin and crime he gave their proper hue,*
> *And hurled at evil what was evil's due.*[10]

He glorified Douglass's courage:

> *He dared the lightning in the lightning's track,*
> *And answered thunder with his thunder back.*[11]

Dunbar also remembered that Douglass was a kind man:

> *His heart, his talents, and his hands were free*
> *To all who truly needed aught [anything] of him.*[12]

Dunbar stated that Frederick Douglass did not save his people from oppression. Rather, he gave them hope that victory was possible. The poem ends with Ethiopia recalling Douglass's message:

> *. . . rising from beneath the chast'ning rod,*
> *She stretches out her bleeding hand to God!*[13]

Dunbar was constantly being pulled in two directions. He needed to work to support himself and his mother, yet he was driven to develop his writing talent. Both goals took time, and the heavy workload caused him deep distress. There were moments when he thought that suicide was the way out. "There is only one thing left to be done, and I am too big a coward to do that," he lamented to a friend.[14]

Dunbar hung on, though. And in 1895, national magazines such as *Munsey's* and *Century* started to print his poems. What's more, he made a new friend who proved to be of great help.

Dr. Henry A. Tobey was a psychiatrist and book lover living in Toledo, Ohio. After reading *Oak and Ivy*, Tobey invited Dunbar to give a recital of his poetry in Toledo. Tobey was distressed to learn of Dunbar's financial burden. Wanting to help this gifted poet, he put up the money to have a second volume of Dunbar's poetry printed. When Dunbar sold this book, there would be no debt to pay back. The new book, *Majors and Minors*, was published in 1896. It contained Dunbar's new work, along with the best poems from *Oak and Ivy*.

Tobey made sure that the reading public paid attention to *Majors and Minors*. He sent copies of the book to some well-known people, such as the actor and playwright James A. Herne, who was performing in Toledo. Herne passed his copy along to William Dean Howells, one of the leading novelists and book critics of his day.

Dunbar's twenty-fourth birthday had just passed when he received a postcard from Tobey urging him to buy the latest issue of *Harper's Weekly*. At first, Dunbar had trouble finding a copy of the magazine. People were snatching it off the newsstands because it was full of news about the nomination of William McKinley for president.

Finally, Dunbar found a copy of *Harper's Weekly* to buy. He stood on the sidewalk reading, ignoring the pedestrians who filed past. Inside the magazine was a glowing review of *Majors and Minors*. Written by William Dean Howells, the review singled out the "minors," the poems written in dialect, for special praise. Howells called Dunbar "the first man of color to study his race objectively, to analyze it to himself, and then to represent it in art as he felt and found it to be; to represent it humorously, yet tenderly, and above all so faithfully that we know the portrait to be undeniably like."[15] *Majors and Minors*, Howells wrote, was a "significant little book."[16]

Two weeks later, Dunbar wrote to thank Howells for

William Dean Howells, a leading novelist and book critic, praised Dunbar's *Majors and Minors*.

the review, saying, "I feel much as a poor, insignificant, helpless boy would feel to suddenly find himself knighted."[17] People all over the country were now reading about Paul Dunbar and *Majors and Minors*. Soon, Dunbar's own name might fly on a banner in fame's bright sky.

5

PEN AND VOICE

n July 1896, Dunbar stepped off a train in a city that was busier and more crowded than any place he had ever seen. New York City was home to more than 3 million people at the end of the nineteenth century, making it the most populous city in the United States. Everywhere, Dunbar heard the hammering of construction. Workers were digging tunnels for subway trains, balancing on steel girders high above the streets, and erecting bridges across New York's rivers. Fashionable people strolled along the city's elegant avenues, while not far away, slum tenements teemed with poverty. Many of the poor were immigrants from Europe. Hundreds of thousands of people were entering the United States at the port of New York every year. One-fourth of them settled in the city, often near other families from their homelands.

African Americans lived in New York City, too. Many had left a life of farming in the South in search of opportunities in the North. Few found those opportunities, though. Denied good jobs and decent housing, they were forced to settle in the Tenderloin district, on the city's West Side. They paid high rents to live in overcrowded buildings. As in other poor neighborhoods of the city, many tenements lacked sewers and running water. Some residents worked hard to make the Tenderloin a better place to live. They organized cultural and political groups, lodges, and church activities. But Dunbar saw too many young people with little hope for the future who turned to a life of crime.

Paul Dunbar had been making some money reciting his poems for audiences in Ohio. He thought that by giving readings in other parts of the country, he could increase his earnings and expose more people to his poetry. William Dean Howells agreed and put Dunbar in touch with Major James Pond, a promoter of concerts and lectures who lived in New York. Pond had arranged public appearances by such famous people as Mark Twain, Frederick Douglass, and Booker T. Washington. Washington was a former slave who had founded the Tuskegee Institute in Alabama, a school

Workers build a bridge over New York City's East River in 1901. The city's growing population needed more buildings and better transportation, and the sounds of construction rang through the streets.

where African Americans could learn such job skills as carpentry and the most up-to-date farming methods.

Major Pond helped Dunbar find an apartment and lined up readings for him throughout the Northeast. Dunbar now mingled in a white world where many people did not know what to make of this black poet. Once, a wealthy woman in Albany, New York, invited him to give a reading in her city and reserved a suite of rooms for him at an exclusive hotel. But Dunbar ran into trouble as soon as he arrived. First, the hotel's desk clerk refused to let him register. Then, the manager threatened to call the police and have Dunbar arrested. It was lucky for Dunbar that the wealthy woman showed up to explain who he was.

Another time, Dunbar performed at Narragansett Pier, Rhode Island, which was a vacation spot for well-to-do whites. An orchestra played as he recited poems such as "The Corn-Stalk Fiddle," which describes a country dance. It was not enough for Dunbar simply to say the lines of poetry out loud. He moved about the stage, taking the parts of the young men and women at the dance and of the musician playing for them on a homemade fiddle:

> *"Salute your partners," comes the call,*
> *"All join hands and circle round,"*
> *"Grand train back," and "Balance all,"*
> *Footsteps lightly spurn the ground.*
> *"Take your lady and balance down the middle"*
> *To the merry strains of the corn-stalk fiddle.*[1]

The elite audience applauded, eager for more.

One well-known person vacationing at Narragansett Pier was Varina Howell Davis. She was the widow of Jefferson Davis, the president of the Southern Confederacy, which fought against the North in the Civil War. She had been unable to attend Dunbar's performance, so she asked him to visit her and to recite some poems as a "special favor."[2] Dunbar politely did as she requested, and she thanked him and praised his work.

How did it make Dunbar feel to perform for the former first lady of a slave-owning nation? People today can only guess at the answer. He behaved with kindness and grace toward Davis, and he never said anything against her. Yet in one bitter poem, "We Wear the Mask," he seems to speak for many African Americans of his day who buried their true feelings when dealing with whites:

> *We wear the mask that grins and lies,*
> *It hides our cheeks and shades our eyes,—*
> *This debt we pay to human guile;*
> *With torn and bleeding hearts we smile . . .*[3]

While Dunbar was giving readings in New York State and New England, Major Pond arranged for Dodd, Mead and Company, a New York–based firm, to publish his next book of poems, *Lyrics of Lowly Life,* and to pay him $400 in advance. This was an important step forward in Dunbar's career. Not only was it helpful to receive so much money, but a large publisher like Dodd, Mead would be able to distribute his book throughout the United States.

Lyrics of Lowly Life was the book that made Paul Laurence Dunbar famous. It sold steadily for the rest of his life, providing needed income. The book contained more than one hundred poems, eleven of which were new. The rest were reprinted from earlier volumes.

William Dean Howells wrote the introduction to the new book and had good things to say about all of Dunbar's work. About the poems in Standard English, he stated, "Some of these I thought very good, and even more than very good. . . ."[4] But, he continued, several other poets could have done just as well. Howells viewed the dialect poems as Dunbar's most important contribution to American literature. He said, "I do not know any one else at present who could quite have written the dialect pieces."[5] Howells said that the dialect poems report "what passes in the hearts and minds of a lowly people. . . ."[6]

Paul Laurence Dunbar was not the first African-American poet to see his work in print. The first published African-American poet is thought to be Jupiter Hammon (1711–1806), who was inspired by the Methodist hymns that he heard in church. African-born Phyllis Wheatley (c. 1753–1784) published her first poem in 1770. Hammon, Wheatley, and others wrote about religion, virtue, and patriotism, much as eighteenth-century white poets were doing. They used the spelling of Standard English and wrote in the same verse forms that white poets employed. Because most African Americans were enslaved at the time and unable to read or buy books, these poets had to please a white reading audience. In the first half of the nineteenth century, poets such as Frances Ellen Watkins Harper (1825–1911) preached against the cruelties of slavery. Harper and the other African-American poets of her time worked closely with the abolitionists, the women and men who were demanding an end to slavery.

The possibility of portraying African-American life in poetry appealed more and more to Dunbar. He had begun to discuss this idea in letters he exchanged with another African-American poet. Alice Ruth Moore was a teacher from New Orleans, Louisiana. Dunbar had read one of her poems in a magazine, where it was printed alongside her picture. The image of the graceful young woman with large, thoughtful eyes captured his attention. He first wrote to her from Dayton in April 1895. "I am drawn to write to you," he said, "because we are both working along the same lines and a sketch of yours in the *Monthly Review* so interested me that I was anxious to know more of you and your work."[7]

Dunbar and Moore exchanged poems and photographs, and they shared their thoughts about writing. They agreed on the need for writers to create characters that are "real live people," whether those characters are white or black.[8] Dunbar stated, "I believe that characters in fiction should be what men and women are in real life—the embodiment of a principle or idea."[9] Before long, he confessed to Moore that she embodied his own ideal. "I love you," he wrote, although he had never met her in person.[10]

"You are an inspiration to me. I am better and purer for having touched hands with you over all these miles."[11] The letter writing continued after Dunbar moved to New York and Moore accepted a teaching job in Boston, Massachusetts.

Dunbar, meanwhile, was preparing to sail to England to give readings of his poetry there. Major Pond's daughter was to travel with him and handle his business affairs. In February 1897, on the night before he departed, friends and well-wishers attended a party in Dunbar's honor. Booker T. Washington, the famous educator, was among the distinguished guests.

It was someone else, though, who made the evening memorable for Dunbar. Alice Moore had slipped away from Boston to come and stand at his side. Well-traveled railroad lines linked Boston and New York, but this was the first time that Dunbar and Moore stood face-to-face. Meeting had been difficult, because Moore's parents disapproved of her friendship with Dunbar. They were snooty members of the black middle class who looked down on Dunbar because he lacked a college education and because his mother had been a laundress. They wanted their daughter to choose a husband with a higher position in society. For that reason, when Moore and Dunbar agreed that night to marry, they kept their plans secret.

Dunbar found England to be free of the racial prejudice that was so common in the United States. In

"I am drawn to write to you," said Dunbar in a letter to Alice
Ruth Moore, after he read one of her poems in a magazine.

England, people accepted him simply as a writer and not as a curiosity. He settled in a tiny attic room, where he looked out on the rooftops and chimneys of London.

The appearances that Major Pond's daughter arranged for him were far different from what Dunbar had expected. Instead of reciting his poems in dignified settings, he was scheduled to perform in variety shows, in between dancing girls and clowns. Sometimes audience members were drunk and rowdy. When he complained to Miss Pond about the drunkenness, she told him to entertain the crowd with vulgar stories! Dunbar was not amused. He wrote to William Dean Howells that he had had his fill of giving readings. He said, "If I can make my living by my pen I will not use my voice."[12]

Dunbar still loved the theater, so he welcomed the chance to work with Samuel Coleridge-Taylor, a composer of English and African descent. Dunbar and Coleridge-Taylor gave two joint recitals of music and poetry. As part of the program, a singer performed some of Dunbar's poems that Coleridge-Taylor had set to music. The two men spent the summer of 1897 writing an operatic play, *Dream Lovers*. It tells the story of a prince from Madagascar who falls in love with a woman he sees in a dream and then searches to find her. Dunbar wrote the entire book—that is, all the dialog and song lyrics—for the show.

The British composer Samuel Coleridge-Taylor, above, set some of Dunbar's poems to music.

With autumn's chill, England felt unfriendly to Paul Dunbar. Miss Pond took off for Paris and left him there alone. He spent many days in his attic room, writing a novel. His first novel, titled *The Uncalled*, concerns a young white man who rebels against his parents' wish for him to become a minister.

For now, Dunbar could not live by his pen alone. His funds were dwindling day by day, so Mr. Dodd of Dodd, Mead and Company sent him the money to come home. Dunbar went back to the nation where he had to wear the grinning mask, and back to Alice Moore.

6

THE CAGED BIRD

When Dunbar returned to the United States in the fall of 1897, a friend helped him secure a job at the Library of Congress in Washington, D.C. The Library of Congress, which is the national library of the United States, is an agency of the federal government. Dunbar settled in LeDroit Park, a fashionable Washington neighborhood near Howard University, the nation's leading traditionally black school. "Come at once," he wrote to his mother at Thanksgiving. "My house is very beautiful and my parlor suite is swell."[1]

Developers built the brick houses of LeDroit Park

Trotting horses pull carriages along LeDroit Park's main thoroughfare. Dunbar moved to this fashionable Washington, D.C., neighborhood in 1897.

in the 1870s to be "far enough away from the noise and bustle of commercial activity to secure quiet and moderate seclusion, yet near enough to enjoy the luxuries of city convenience," as they stated in their advertising brochure.[2] At first, the developers sold their houses to white families only. African Americans began moving to LeDroit Park in the 1890s.

Alice Moore was now teaching in Brooklyn, New York. In March 1898, Dunbar traveled to New York City, where he and Alice were secretly married. Dunbar had told only one person, his mother, about his wedding plans. His friends learned of the marriage in April, when the couple mailed out announcements.

As soon as the school year was over, Alice Dunbar left her teaching post in Brooklyn and joined her husband in Washington. Like other communities throughout the South, the nation's capital was a segregated city. Black and white Washingtonians ate in separate restaurants and sat in separate waiting rooms at railroad stations. Black and white children attended different schools. In 1896, in deciding a case known as *Plessy* v. *Ferguson*, the U.S. Supreme Court had determined that such segregation was legal as long as the two races enjoyed services that were "separate but equal." But the services available to blacks were nearly always inferior to those provided to whites.

Despite segregation, Washington was home to many accomplished African Americans, including doctors, lawyers, teachers, and ministers. The Dunbars enjoyed a busy social life filled with teas and card parties, concerts and book discussions. In the summer, they vacationed with friends on the shore of Chesapeake Bay in Maryland. "Here exists a society which is sufficient unto itself," Dunbar noted, "a society which is satisfied with its own condition, and which is not asking for social intercourse with whites."[3]

The newlyweds lived next door to Mary Church Terrell, whom Dunbar had met at the World's Columbian Exposition in Chicago. Terrell was teaching foreign languages at the Washington high school where her husband was principal. She had become the first African American to serve on the Washington, D.C., school board. In 1896, she had helped to form the National Association of Colored Women.

Terrell and Dunbar now renewed their friendship. They talked many times about poetry and art, and Dunbar showed her his newest poems. Years later, Terrell recalled those visits with her old friend. "I can see Paul Dunbar beckoning me, as I walked by, when he wanted to read me a poem which he had just written or when he wished to discuss a word or a subject on which he had not fully decided," she wrote. "Paul often came to see me to read his poems or his prose articles before he sent them to magazines."[4]

The years in Washington were a fruitful time in Dunbar's writing career. His first novel, *The Uncalled,* was published in 1898, and so was his short-story collection *Folks from Dixie*. Dunbar based some of the stories in that book on his conversations with former slaves about life in the past. In others, he dealt with problems that faced the African Americans of his day. For example, the story "Jimsella" describes the difficulties that a young husband and wife from the South face as they make a new life for themselves in a northern city. Living in a tiny tenement apartment without enough money to buy good food and decent clothing strains the couple's marriage. "Aunt Mandy's Investment," another story, presents the unpleasant fact that many poor African Americans in cities were being swindled by dishonest members of their own race.

In 1899, Dunbar published two books of poetry, *Lyrics of the Hearthside* and *Poems of Cabin and Field*. Once again, the books contained some poems in Standard English and some in dialect. Poems such as "Little Brown Baby" present warm scenes of family life:

> *Little brown baby wif spa'klin' eyes,*
> *Come to yo' pappy an' set on his knee.*
> *What you been doin', suh—makin' san' pies?*
> *Look at dat bib—you's ez du'ty ez me.*[5]

The father in this poem regrets that he cannot protect his child from life's sorrows and hardships:

> *Wisht you could allus know ease an' cleah skies;*
> *Wisht you could stay jes' a chile on my breas'—*
> *Little brown baby wif spa'klin' eyes!*[6]

Dunbar also had written a poem in memory of Alexander Crummell, the tireless missionary who promoted the concept of pan-Africanism, and who died in 1898. Calling Crummell "Child of the earth,"[7] Dunbar asked in his poem, "Who shall come after thee, out of the clay— / Learned one and leader to show us the way?"[8]

Another poem pays tribute to Harriet Beecher Stowe (1811–1896), the author of *Uncle Tom's Cabin*. In that famous novel, which was first issued as a book in 1852, Stowe vividly described the cruelties of slavery. *Uncle Tom's Cabin* persuaded many Americans living in northern states to work to end slavery. For that reason, its publication was one of the factors leading to the Civil War. Dunbar wrote about Stowe:

> *She told the story, and the whole world wept*
> *At wrongs and cruelties it had not known*
> *But for this fearless woman's voice alone.*[9]

The critics ignored the fine poems in Standard English, though. They all seemed to follow the lead of William Dean Howells and to prefer the works in dialect. The white reading public—the majority of readers in the United States—had formed a narrow opinion about the kind of poetry that an African American should write.

Alice Dunbar explained that the poems in Standard English meant much more to her husband than the dialect poetry did. Although he portrayed African-

American life in his dialect work, she said, "it was in the pure English poems that the poet expressed *himself*."[10] She said that the Standard English poetry contained "his dearest dreams."[11] Alice Dunbar also said about her husband, "He never spoke in dialect."[12]

The well-being of all African Americans concerned Paul Dunbar. In 1890, he followed the news about African-American fighting men who were serving heroically in the Spanish-American War. This brief war took place on the island of Cuba, ninety miles south of Florida. Cuba had been a colony of Spain since 1511. For several years, though, the Cubans had been struggling for independence. Americans hoped to see a Cuban victory, because they disliked having a European colony so close to their shores. They also objected to the cruel treatment of Cubans by Spanish military forces.

The United States sent a battleship, the U.S.S. *Maine*, to Havana Harbor, Cuba, in a show of support. On the night of February 15, 1898, a huge explosion sank the *Maine* and killed 266 people. To this day, no one knows the cause of the explosion, but in 1898, many Americans placed the blame on Spain. Congress passed a resolution calling for Spain to leave Cuba. But the Spanish stayed, and the United States and Spain went to war.

Four units of African-American soldiers were among the United States forces sent to Cuba. These men, who were sometimes called Buffalo Soldiers, had served with distinction on the western frontier of the United States. A future president, Theodore Roosevelt, also fought in the Spanish-American War. He led a band of cowboys and adventurers known as the Rough Riders.

Soon after reaching Cuba in June, the Buffalo Soldiers rescued some Rough Riders who were being attacked by Spanish sharpshooters. On July 1, the African Americans helped to win the Battle of San Juan Hill, the most important conflict in the war. The body count from that battle was high. One fifth of the African Americans who fought at San Juan Hill lost their lives. Ten African Americans received the Medal of Honor, the nation's highest military award, for their actions in Cuba.

While those African Americans received praise from their leaders, others were being murdered by their neighbors. On February 22, 1898, a white mob set fire to the post office in Lake City, South Carolina, and to the home of the town's black postmaster. The flames and smoke woke up the postmaster, his wife, and their six children. Before the family could escape, the mob began shooting into the house. A report in the Cleveland, Ohio, *Gazette* described what happened next:

> The postmaster was the first to reach the door and he fell dead just within the threshold, being shot in

several places. The mother had the baby in her arms and reached the door over her husband's body, when a bullet crashed through [the baby's] skull, and it fell to the floor. [The mother] was shot in several places. Two of the girls had their arms broken close to the shoulders and will probably lose them. Another of the girls is fatally wounded. The boy was also shot.[13]

Southern whites did not want blacks to attain high positions in the community, and they did not want blacks to vote or hold public office. In Wilmington, North Carolina, on November 10, 1898, a white supremacist group called the Red Shirts started a race riot. The immediate cause was a rumor that the city's African Americans were secretly arming themselves with guns. The underlying cause was racial tension that had been building for many months. African Americans were in the majority in Wilmington, but the white population was growing. Most of the business and professional people were African American, and African Americans served on the city council. A crowd of resentful whites destroyed the office of a black-owned newspaper. The crowd murdered eleven African Americans and wounded many more. No one was punished for these crimes. In fact, the leader of the white terrorists was elected mayor of Wilmington.

Paul Dunbar understood the attitude of many whites to be this: "Negroes, you may fight for us, but you may not vote for us. . . . You may be heroes in war, but you must be cravens [cowards] in peace."[14] In an

The well-being of all African Americans concerned Paul
Laurence Dunbar.

essay written after the Wilmington riots, he condemned the behavior of those whites. He reminded the nation that "the question is not one of the Negro's fitness to rule or to vote, but of the right of the whites to murder him for the sake of instruction."[15] Dunbar declared, "For so long a time has the black man believed that he is an American citizen that he will not be easily convinced to the contrary. It will take more than the hangings, the burnings and the lynchings, both North and South, to prove it to his satisfaction."[16]

Dunbar was working very hard. He was turning out stories, poems, and essays, and he was traveling to other cities to give readings. And he still held down his job at the Library of Congress. He had no interest in the medical and scientific books that he catalogued and shelved all day. The dull job dampened his spirits, but he needed his salary to support his wife and his mother. "The iron gratings of the book stacks in the Library of Congress suggested to him the bars of the bird's cage," Alice Dunbar wrote.[17] She said that the hot Washington summer made Dunbar wish for the freedom to loaf beside a river in Dayton. "The dry dust of the dry books . . . rasped sharply in his hot throat; and he understood how the bird felt when it beat its wings against its cage."[18] That experience, Alice Dunbar claimed, caused her husband to write "Sympathy," one of his best-loved poems:

Paul Laurence Dunbar

I know what the caged bird feels, alas!
   When the sun is bright on the upland slopes;
When the wind stirs soft through the springing grass,
And the river flows like a stream of glass;
When the first bird sings and the first bud opes,
And the faint perfume from its chalice steals—
I know what the caged bird feels!

I know why the caged bird beats his wing
   Till its blood is red on the cruel bars;
For he must fly back to his perch and cling
When he fain would be on the bough a-swing;
   And a pain still throbs in the old, old scars
And they pulse again with a keener sting—
I know why he beats his wing!

I know why the caged bird sings, ah me,
   When his wing is bruised and his bosom sore,—
When he beats his bars and he would be free;
It is not a carol of joy or glee,
   But a prayer that he sends from his heart's deep core,
But a plea, that upward to heaven he flings—
I know why the caged bird sings![19]

7

AN UNKNOWN COUNTRY

Mary Church Terrell was not the only old friend Paul Dunbar met again in Washington, D.C. The violinist Will Marion Cook was living there as well. Cook had studied classical music in Europe and in New York City, but no orchestra would hire him because of his race. Instead of giving up his dream of a musical career, Cook found a different way to use his talent. He was writing his own musical arrangements of African-American folk songs and popular music.

Early in 1898, Cook told Dunbar that he'd had a "tremendous idea": He was going to write a musical show that told the story of the cakewalk.[1] The cakewalk is a dance that originated among enslaved African Americans. It is thought that the slaves were poking fun at the stiff posture and formal behavior of whites attending fancy dress balls. In the late nineteenth century, the cakewalk gained popularity as a dance contest in which the winning couple received a cake. Cook knew that he could write the music for the show with no trouble, but he needed help with the dialog and song lyrics. He asked Dunbar to work with him.

Dunbar had several reasons to refuse. For one

Couples take their places as an elegant cakewalk dance is about to begin. In 1898, Dunbar was asked to write the lyrics for a musical show about this dance craze.

thing, he was already up to his ears in work. After spending his days at the Library of Congress, he stayed up late writing poetry at night. The workload was straining his marriage. For another, he was not feeling well. Finally, his wife disapproved of the project.

To Alice Dunbar, Cook's musical sounded like a minstrel show, and she did not want her husband working on a show that made fun of African Americans. Minstrel shows came about in the first half of the nineteenth century. White performers darkened their faces with makeup and danced, sang, played musical instruments, and told jokes. They based their acts on stereotypes, or widely held beliefs, about the way that all African Americans behaved. African-American entertainers began joining minstrel shows after the Civil War. They, too, wore dark makeup and conformed to the stereotypes, but not by choice. For many, this was the only way to get a job in the theater.

Will Marion Cook explained that he had something very different in mind. He planned to hire the best African American performers and give them a chance to show their ability in a way that was not demeaning. Cook kept asking Dunbar to participate, and at last Dunbar consented.

The writing went quickly. Cook and Dunbar stayed awake one night to draft the show. "Without a piano or anything but the kitchen table, we finished all the songs, all the libretto [the lyrics and spoken words] and all but a few bars of the ensembles by four o'clock the next morning," Cook remembered.[2]

Clorindy, the Origin of the Cakewalk opened that summer at the Casino Roof Garden in New York City. Many of the theaters along New York's Broadway had gardens and smaller stages on their roofs. After the show downstairs ended, the audience went to the roof for more entertainment. *Clorindy* may not have been the main attraction at the Casino Theater, but it was a huge hit. Will Marion Cook never forgot the first performance. He stated, "At the finish of the opening chorus, the applause and cheering were so tumultuous that I simply stood there transfixed, my hand in the air, unable to move. . . ."[3] People today would call some of the show's songs and characters offensive to African Americans, but in 1898 they marked a step forward. The audience liked one musical number so much that the singer repeated it ten times.

Dunbar and Cook wrote a second musical play, *Uncle Eph's Christmas*, which starred Ernest Hogan, one of the leading African-American comedians of the 1890s. This show, which was first performed in 1899, clearly contained the minstrel-show humor that Alice Dunbar hated. After listening to his wife's objections, Dunbar regretted having worked on the play. He met with Cook and the actors and asked to withdraw his name from the show. The discussion went well until Alice Dunbar spoke up. She got into an argument with

Will Marion Cook's musical arrangements used tunes and rhythms from African-American folk songs and popular music. Cook, above, and Dunbar created musical plays with Cook's music and Dunbar's lyrics.

Ernest Hogan, angered her husband, and quarreled with him as well. Back home in Washington, friends were gossiping about the Dunbars, whispering that their fights were becoming more frequent.

Paul Dunbar was traveling as much as ever to give readings throughout the East and the Midwest. He had resigned from his job at the Library of Congress in January 1899. That spring, he saw the South for the first time when the board of trustees of Atlanta University awarded him an honorary master of arts degree. He also visited the Tuskegee Normal and Industrial Institute in Alabama, the school for African Americans founded by Booker T. Washington.

Washington believed that African Americans could get ahead in society only gradually, by making themselves useful to whites. His school taught the students ways to earn a living with their hands. Washington said that only in the years to come, after their race had gained the acceptance of whites, could African Americans reach higher to become artists, writers, and scholars. In 1895, he told a white audience in Atlanta, Georgia, that whites and blacks in the United States could be "as separate as the five fingers" in their social lives even as blacks advanced economically.[4] Other African-American leaders challenged Washington's viewpoint. They argued that he was giving in to white prejudice and ignoring the harm that discrimination caused.

Dunbar liked Booker T. Washington, and the two men got along well. Dunbar toured the school, and he talked to the advanced classes about writing. He met the famous scientist George Washington Carver, who was conducting research at Tuskegee on new uses for the peanut. In 1901, Dunbar would write the lyrics for Tuskegee's school song.

But Dunbar never accepted Washington's ideas about the education of African Americans. He was convinced that manual training might be helpful for some members of his race, but not for everyone. Well before he saw the Tuskegee Institute, Dunbar had remarked, "I do not believe that a young man, whose soul is turbulent with a message which should be given to the world through the pulpit or the press, should shut his mouth and shoe horses. . . ."[5] He saw himself as that young man, and he said, "I should have been very unhappy if condemned to follow a handicraft."[6] Dunbar warned that "educating the hand to the exclusion of the head" was a dangerous practice.[7] He preferred to see every person work to achieve his or her dreams.

In this way, Dunbar's thinking was more like that of the great intellectual W. E. B. Du Bois. Du Bois spoke about the "Talented Tenth," the most gifted 10 percent of the African-American population. He said that this group should attain the highest level of education possible and could then act as leaders in the African-

American community. Responding to Booker T. Washington's speech in Atlanta, Du Bois stated, "Negroes must insist continually, in season and out of season, . . . that black boys need education as well as white boys."[8]

Dunbar next boarded a train to go north. Theodore Roosevelt, who was governor of New York in 1899, had asked Dunbar to speak at a conference in Albany, the state capital. Dunbar still felt unwell, though, and he never made it to the conference. He collapsed on a railroad platform while changing trains in New York City and was transported to a hospital. There, doctors determined that he had pneumonia, an infection in his lungs.

Alice Dunbar rushed to New York to nurse her husband through the illness. But she could do little more than make him comfortable. Before the discovery of antibiotics, pneumonia killed about a third of its victims. In order to save his life, the physicians performed surgery on Dunbar to drain fluid from his lungs. Then, gradually, he began to feel better.

The doctors prescribed rest, so the Dunbars spent some time in the Catskill Mountains of New York State. In September, they went west to Denver, Colorado, hoping that the city's dry air would benefit Dunbar's lungs.

Denver was unlike any city that Dunbar had seen in the East. The place that in the 1850s had been a group of temporary settlements was now the capital of

A young man learns the trade of mattress making at Booker T. Washington's Tuskegee Institute. Dunbar wrote the lyrics for Tuskegee's school song, but he never agreed with Washington's ideas about education.

Colorado. Residents bragged about their new railroad station built of stone, with its large, circular waiting room. They showed visitors the domed state capitol, a building that had cost $1.5 million to construct. Denver had a university, an opera house, luxury hotels, and an observatory for studying the stars. Smelting plants operated day and night to process the gold and silver ore dug from the many mines in the region. In the distance, the Dunbars could see the Rocky Mountains—Long's Peak to the northwest, Gray's Peak to the west, and Pike's Peak to the southwest.

Denver inspired Dunbar's second novel, *The Love of Landry*, which was published in 1900. This novel tells of a young woman who goes west to improve her health and falls in love with a cowboy. In describing the woman's struggle to get well, Dunbar showed that he understood the loneliness and fear that so often accompany serious illness. The sick person enters "an unknown, uncared-for country," he wrote, "there to fight, hand to hand with death, an uncertain fight."[9] The battle never lets up, Dunbar observed. It rages "in the still night, when all the world's asleep, in the gray day, in the pale morning . . ."[10]

In 1900, Dunbar also published a short-story collection, *The Strength of Gideon and Other Stories*. He wrote again about the problems of African Americans from the South who were living in northern cities. In the story "An Old-Time Christmas," a homesick woman is saddened when her teenaged son starts gambling and gets into trouble with the police. She feels he would not have faced the same temptations in the rural South.

Paul and Alice Dunbar remained in Denver through the winter and spring. They returned to Washington as the hot summer of 1900 was approaching. Once more, Dunbar consulted a doctor, and this time he learned the true cause of his ill health. He had tuberculosis, an infectious disease that commonly affects the lungs and that claimed many lives in the nineteenth and early twentieth centuries. The doctor insisted on bed rest, and he prescribed whiskey, as was the custom at that time, to boost Dunbar's energy.

Never in his life had Paul Dunbar sat still for long, though. In August, he went to New York to patch up his friendship with Ernest Hogan. He stopped in at the offices of Dodd, Mead and Company to collect the earnings from his books. It was money he truly needed. Then he went to the Tenderloin district and headed straight into trouble.

On August 12, a black resident of the city named Arthur Harris had fought with a white man, a plain-clothes police officer. Harris insisted that he had been defending his wife, but he had used a knife in the fight, and the police officer was dead. On the evening of August 15, an angry mob of whites descended on the Tenderloin and attacked every black person in their path. The whites pulled African Americans from streetcars and beat them. The police offered black residents no protection. In fact, they sided with the whites and clubbed and kicked blacks. The rioting continued, off and on, for three days.

In an unhappy twist of fate, August 15 was the date Dunbar chose for his visit to the Tenderloin. He escaped without injury, but he was robbed of his money. He had no choice but to work harder than ever, to give more readings, and to move deeper into that unknown country, illness.

8

No Rest

ore and more, Paul Dunbar turned to whiskey to improve his health. It failed to do any good, though. Instead of getting better, he became dependent on alcohol to get through the day.

The public learned how serious Dunbar's drinking problem was in October 1900, when he was scheduled to give a recital at a church in Evanston, Illinois. The audience in the church hall waited a long time for Dunbar to appear. At last he arrived, escorted by a nurse and a doctor. The performer who once had been full of energy now walked unsteadily to the front of the hall. His voice sounded thin, and he slurred his words. People who remembered Dunbar's strong speaking voice now had to strain to hear him. The audience saw that Dunbar was drunk. One by one, people walked out of the church.

The National Women's Christian Temperance Union, a group that promoted abstinence from alcohol, had its headquarters in Evanston. People there had less tolerance for drunkenness than people did in other cities. Dunbar regretted his behavior at the recital, especially when a local newspaper reported on the event. Alice Dunbar read the news article and found another reason to be angry with her husband.

Dunbar's tuberculosis had progressed, and he often coughed up blood. Yet he continued to live a fast-paced life. He still gave poetry readings, and he wrote poems, stories, and magazine articles. In 1901, he published *The Fanatics*, a novel that explores attitudes about race at the time of the Civil War. Dunbar wrote about a young white couple in a northern town, Robert Van Doren and Mary Waters. The two are forbidden to marry because Robert's family favors the Confederate cause in the Civil War and Mary's family supports the Union. The two families resolve their differences, but the Waterses reveal that their concern for African Americans has limits. Although they are against slavery, they object strongly when escaped slaves move to their town.

Dunbar wrote another novel, *The Sport of the Gods*, in just one month. Some experts have called this book Dunbar's most realistic look at African-American life. *The Sport of the Gods* is set at the start of the twentieth century, the time when Dunbar was writing it. It is a novel about family and community ties, and what happens to people when those ties are broken. It tells the story of Berry Hamilton, an African-American butler working for a white family in the South. Berry is wrongly accused of stealing money and is sent to prison. His wife, Fannie, and their grown children, Joe and Kitty, are promptly turned out of their home. The whites in town refuse to hire them. The black community rejects the Hamiltons, too. It was dangerous for blacks to disagree with white opinion in a small southern town.

With no friends, and thinking they will never see Berry again, the Hamiltons move to New York City. They are unprepared for the streetwise people and the temptations that they encounter. Joe is led into a life of drinking and crime, and Kitty becomes a showgirl. Wrongly believing that Berry's jail term amounts to a divorce, Fannie marries an abusive gambler. Berry Hamilton is freed from prison and finds his family at last. Dunbar concludes that his characters went on to live a life that was only partly happy, "but it was all that was left to them, and they took it up without complaint. . . ."[1]

Paul Laurence Dunbar was a well-known figure in American life. President William McKinley invited the African-American poet to ride a horse in his inaugural parade on March 4, 1901. McKinley, who had been elected to a second term as president, gave Dunbar the honorary rank of colonel for the day. Soon after the parade, Dunbar went to Jacksonville, Florida, where he observed, "Down here one finds my poems recited everywhere."[2] Young African-American men earned money for college by reading Dunbar's poetry in public. Children performed his poems for tourists at resort hotels to raise funds for their schools.

Dunbar was in Florida to give readings himself and to see his old friend James Weldon Johnson. Johnson, who was employed as a school principal, hoped that a long rest in Florida's warm climate would do the poet some good. During the six weeks that Dunbar spent at the Johnson home, the two men talked often about poetry. Dunbar, in his illness, felt bitter toward the readers who liked only his poems in dialect. He said to Johnson, "You know, of course, that I didn't start as a dialect poet. I simply came to the conclusion that I could write it as well, if not better, than anybody else I knew of, and that by doing so I should gain a hearing, . . . and now they don't want me to write anything but dialect."[3]

Dunbar had even expressed his frustration in rhyme, in "The Poet":

Dunbar's friend and fellow writer James Weldon Johnson. "His voice was a perfect instrument and he knew how to use it," said Johnson of Dunbar's poetry readings.

> *He sang of love when earth was young,*
> *And Love, itself, was in his lays.*
> *But ah, the world, it turned to praise*
> *A jingle in a broken tongue.*[4]

Johnson hated to hear Dunbar belittle his work. He reminded his friend that the dialect poems had value. "The thing that I was sure of and kept repeating to him," Johnson said, "was that he had carried traditional dialect poetry as far and as high as it could go; that he had brought to it the fullest measure of charm, tenderness, and beauty it could hold."[5]

Dunbar hinted to Johnson that he wanted to write more poems in Standard English, perhaps including some very long poems that described events in African-American history.

It surprised Johnson to see how rapidly Dunbar could write, even when he was so ill. Dunbar completed one poem after another in Florida. "As quickly as he finished them he sent them off; two of them, I remember, to the *Saturday Evening Post* [a weekly magazine]; and I was amazed at seeing how promptly he received checks in return. Whatever he wrote was in demand," Johnson noted.[6]

Dunbar did manage to relax during the visit, though. Every night before going to bed, he ate a raw onion and drank a glass of beer. He insisted that the strange snack was good for his health. Also, he got to know Johnson's brother, J. Rosamond Johnson, a

composer who had studied at the New England
Conservatory, one of the nation's leading music
schools. In 1900, the Johnson brothers had written the
song "Lift Every Voice and Sing," which is known as
the African-American national anthem. Now Rosamond
Johnson set some of Dunbar's poetry to music, including "Li'l' Gal," one of his newest dialect poems:

> *Dere's a hummin' an' a bummin'*
> *in de lan' f'om eas' to wes',*
> *I's a-sighin' fu' you, honey, an' I*
> *nevah know no res'.*
> *Fu' dey's lots o' trouble brewin'*
> *an' a-stewin' in my breas',*
> *Li'l' gal.*[7]

Rosamond Johnson's setting of "Li'l' Gal" remained
popular with Americans for many years.

Dunbar returned to Washington, D.C., and as soon
as the weather turned summery, he and Alice headed
for the Chesapeake Bay. But the fun of previous vaca-
tions on the Maryland shore was missing this time.
Both of the Dunbars were bitten by disease carrying
mosquitoes and came down with malaria, an illness
that causes chills, fever, and sweating. Any happiness
that had remained in their marriage now seemed to be
gone. Alice Dunbar wrote to her mother-in-law, "We
quarrel all the time."[8]

On New Year's Day, 1902, Paul Dunbar attended a
reception at the White House as a guest of the new

president. Theodore Roosevelt had been William McKinley's vice president. After McKinley was assassinated in Buffalo, New York, in September 1901, the forty-two-year-old Roosevelt had become the youngest president in U.S. history.

Later that January, Dunbar journeyed to South Carolina to give a poetry reading. He argued with Alice upon his return, and she ordered him to leave their house. Paul Dunbar marched out in a fury, and he never saw his wife again.

9

BACK HOME

aul Dunbar went to New York City, where he teamed up once more with Will Marion Cook. Dunbar and Cook wrote another musical play, *In Dahomey*, in which two detectives from Boston are hired to find a lost silver chest. The search takes the detectives all the way to Africa. (Dahomey is the former name of Benin, a republic in West Africa.)

The new show was a huge success, both in New York and in England. It was performed at Buckingham Palace, the home of the British royal family in London, as a birthday treat for the Prince of Wales. But Dunbar found no joy in this achievement. His health was too

Comedian Bert Williams starred in Dunbar's musical play *In Dahomey*. Like many African-American performers of his day, Williams darkened his face with makeup.

poor, and he felt heartsick over his separation from Alice. Everything and everyone seemed to get on his nerves. He complained to James Weldon Johnson that he would never write another show with Will Marion Cook. He said, "I just can't work with Cook; he irritates me beyond endurance."[1]

Dunbar did whatever he could think of to repair his broken marriage. He sent letters and telegrams to Alice in Washington. He traveled to Boston, where she once had lived, and asked her friends there to persuade Alice to see him. Nothing he tried did any good, though. Alice answered none of his messages, and she refused to listen to any talk about getting back together. She was making a new life for herself as a teacher in Washington, D.C.

In 1902, a broken Paul Dunbar moved to Chicago, to be near his half-brother Robert. He did not stay for long. The city that had excited him in 1893, when he was twenty-one and healthy, now tired him. Its streets were too noisy and crowded for a sick man. Before the year was over, Dunbar left Chicago for Dayton, where he lived with his mother in a house on North Summit Street. His childhood friend Bud Burns, who was now a physician, came often to care for him.

His birthplace soothed him as no other city could. In the poem "Bein' Back Home," Dunbar wrote about the comfort of well-known surroundings for someone who is ill:

Paul Laurence Dunbar

"He sang of love when earth was young . . . ," wrote Dunbar in "The Poet."

Kind o' nice to set aroun'
On the old familiar groun',
Knowin' that when Death does come,
That he'll find you right at home.[2]

Paul Dunbar may have gone home, but he did little "setting around." He wore himself out giving readings throughout the Midwest and the East, in places as distant from one another as Lawrence, Kansas, and Baltimore, Maryland.

In 1903, he published a new book of poetry, *Lyrics of Love and Laughter.* One of its poems, "Black Samson of Brandywine," describes the brave feats of an African-American soldier in a Revolutionary War battle that took place near Chadds Ford, Pennsylvania, on September 11, 1777. Historians know little about the hero remembered as Black Samson, who was one of five thousand African Americans who fought in the American Revolution. But Dunbar cared more about the man's courage than about the details of his life. He wrote:

Was he a freeman or bondman [slave]?
Was he a man or a thing?
What does it matter? His brav'ry
Renders him royal—a king.[3]

In the poem "Dinah Kneading Dough," Dunbar revealed the beauty to be found in everyday life as he described an African-American woman making bread:

Brown arms buried elbow deep
Their domestic rhythm keep,
As with steady sweep they go
Through the gently yielding dough.
Maids may vaunt [brag about] their finer charms—
Naught to me like Dinah's arms;
Girls may draw, or paint, or sew—
I love Dinah kneading dough.[4]

Lyrics of Love and Laughter also contained the touching poem "Life's Tragedy," in which Dunbar expressed a thought that he would later repeat to his closest friends. He regretted that he had never achieved all he had hoped to as a writer:

To have come near to sing the perfect song
*   And only by a half-tone lost the key,*
There is the potent sorrow, there the grief;
*   The pale, sad staring of life's tragedy.*[5]

In 1904, a new book of short stories by Paul Laurence Dunbar arrived at America's bookstores. It was titled *The Heart of Happy Hollow*. Dunbar stated in the book's preface that he had written about ordinary African Americans, people who lived in "the cities or villages, north or south, wherever the hod carrier [bricklayer's helper], the porter and the waiter are the society men of the town."[6] Dunbar's stories gave readers a window into the lives of men who had spent decades preaching the Gospel and of women who took in laundry, as his mother had done. The "Happy Hollow" that Dunbar described was not always a merry place, as stories such as "The Lynching of Jubc Benson" pointed out.

These stories reflected the harsh reality of life in the United States for African Americans. A plague of race riots afflicted the nation in the early twentieth century. One of the grisliest riots occurred in Statesboro, Georgia, in August 1904, after the bodies of a white farm family were discovered. Local officials arrested two black men and charged them with the murders. They hastily tried the men and convicted them. As soon as the judge sentenced the two men to hang, an angry white mob rushed into the courtroom and snatched the prisoners. Courtroom guards did nothing as the mob dragged the men outside and burned them alive.

More violence followed. The mob moved through town, attacking African Americans and destroying their homes. One man was severely whipped for riding his bicycle on a sidewalk. The mother of a newborn baby received a beating and saw her husband murdered. Not one white was punished for the crimes in Statesboro.

The rioting spread beyond the South. Another disturbance took place in Springfield, Ohio, a city near Dayton. Once again, whites took the law into their own hands and murdered a black man who was in police custody. An enraged crowd of whites attacked black residents and burned homes and businesses on the black side of town.

Paul Laurence Dunbar was one Ohioan living in peace and quiet. He spent his days at home now, writing. Although it tired him out to hold a pen, he completed a final book of verse, *Lyrics of Sunshine and Shadow*, which was published in 1905. Dunbar was only thirty-two years old, but the poems are those of a person who has reached the end of life. Some, such as "Compensation," talk about failure in love and work:

> *Because I have loved so vainly,*
> *And sung with such faltering breath,*
> *The Master in infinite mercy*
> *Offers the boon of Death.*[7]

Dunbar was clearly weakening. The friends who visited him were shocked at his appearance. "When I saw him then, he was wasted and worn by disease and he was coughing his precious young life away," wrote Mary Church Terrell.[8] She was in Dayton to address the Ohio State Federation of Colored Women's Clubs and had come to see her old friend and neighbor. Some young women dropped in to chat with Dunbar while she was there. To cheer him up, Terrell joked, "Sometimes I am tempted to believe you are not half so ill as you pretend to be. I believe you are just playing the role of interesting invalid, so as to receive the sympathy and homage of those beautiful girls."[9]

Paul Laurence Dunbar, late in life, at home among his photographs and mementos.

Dunbar laughed and said, "Sometimes I think I'm just loafing myself."[10]

He was much more somber when he talked to James Weldon Johnson about the long poems on African-American history that remained unwritten. "I've kept on doing the same things, and doing them no better," he said. "I have never gotten to the things I really wanted to do."[11]

As Thanksgiving approached, Dunbar grew frailer. He rarely left the house. He did venture out, though, on a November day to attend the funeral of Bud Burns. His friend and doctor had died suddenly after a brief illness. About his day-to-day doings, Dunbar wrote to an acquaintance, "My life consists of going to bed at the beginning of the month and staying there, with very brief intervals of half an hour or so, until the beginning of the next month."[12]

By New Year's Day, 1906, the sad end was in sight. Matilda Dunbar watched over her son as he labored to breathe and slipped in and out of consciousness. On February 9, she sent for a doctor and a minister. As the doctor tried to make the sick man more comfortable, the minister recited the Twenty-third Psalm from the Bible. Dunbar awakened briefly to speak some of the words: "Yea though I walk through the valley of the shadow . . ."[13] And then his voice fell silent. He died at 3:30 that winter afternoon at the age of thirty-three.

10

SINGING TO
THE DAWN

n February 12, Lincoln's birthday, in 1906, the friends and loved ones of Paul Laurence Dunbar came together at the Eaker Street African Methodist Episcopal Church in Dayton to say a last good-bye. Two floral tributes blanketed Dunbar's casket, an arrangement of white lilacs and lilies from James Whitcomb Riley and a spray of American beauty roses from Central High School. The leaders of Dayton's African-American community were on hand; one of them praised "the invaluable service rendered by Dunbar to his race, the nation, and to the world of letters. . . ."[1] Dunbar's longtime friend Dr. Tobey could barely speak through his tears. "I never loved a man so much," he said.[2]

Paul Laurence Dunbar was laid to rest in Woodlawn Cemetery, near an ancient oak tree. The citizens of Dayton placed a monument on his grave that is inscribed with lines from his poem "A Death Song":

Lay me down beneaf de willers in de grass,
Whah de branch [stream] 'll go a-singin' as it pass.
*   An' w'en I's a-layin' low,*
*   I kin hyeah it as it go*
Singin', "Sleep, my honey, tek yo' res' at las'."[3]

Black and white Americans alike mourned the loss of Paul Laurence Dunbar. Recalling the poet soon after his death, Mary Church Terrell wrote,

Because he has lived and wrought [worked], the race to which he belonged has been lifted to a high plane. Each and every person in the United States remotely identified with his race is held in higher esteem because of the ability which Paul Dunbar possessed and the success he undoubtedly attained.[4]

Brand Whitlock, the mayor of Toledo, had admired Dunbar, too. He praised Dunbar in a letter to Dr. Tobey that was read aloud at the funeral. Whitlock wrote that "Paul was a poet; and I find that when I have said that I have said the greatest and most splendid thing that can be said about a man."[5] Whitlock observed that Dunbar was a poet "not of his own race alone. . . . but the poet of you and me and of all men everywhere."[6]

Matilda Dunbar lived into her nineties. In 1938, after she had died, the state of Ohio dedicated the Dunbar home on North Summit Street in Dayton as a public shrine. The house is now a museum where readers of Dunbar's books can learn more about the man who wrote them. Alice Dunbar married again. She continued to write, and she edited two books that contain writings by Paul Laurence Dunbar, *Masterpieces of Negro Eloquence* (1914) and *The Dunbar Speaker and Entertainer* (1920).

In 1906, the year Dunbar died, W. E. B. Du Bois and other African-American thinkers met at Harper's Ferry, West Virginia. They were holding the first open meeting of the Niagara Movement, an organization formed secretly near Niagara Falls, Canada, in 1905. Its purposes were to rid society of racial discrimination and to promote equal treatment under the law. The Niagara Movement existed for five years, until it was eclipsed by the National Association for the Advancement of Colored People (NAACP), which was founded in New York City in 1909 and remains active today.

The reading public took a greater interest in books by African-American authors in the years following Dunbar's death. Writers and artists gathered in urban areas, such as Harlem in New York City, where they strove to depict African-American life in their work. This flourishing of the arts, which is often called the

Harlem Renaissance, occurred roughly from 1918 through the late 1930s, between the two world wars. The poets of this period, notably James Weldon Johnson, Claude McKay, and Langston Hughes, owed a debt to Paul Laurence Dunbar. He had succeeded at a time when there were no older African-American writers to guide him. He pointed the way for others.

The next generation of writers also learned from Dunbar. In 1940, Richard Wright published his first novel, *Native Son*. It tells the story of Bigger Thomas, a young African American who is driven to crime by the pressures of a racist society. Wright explored his characters' minds much more deeply than Dunbar ever did. But anyone who has read the story of Joe Hamilton in *The Sport of the Gods* can detect the influence of Paul Laurence Dunbar on Richard Wright.

Dunbar's popularity waned in the 1940s and 1950s. Literary critics—people who study poetry and fiction—objected to his dialect poems. They perceived that Dunbar wrote in dialect to please white readers at the expense of his race. It became fashionable to dismiss Paul Laurence Dunbar, likening his work to that of the white plantation poet Irwin Russell. Still, many of the same critics praised the writings of Mark Twain (1835–1910), who used both white and black dialect in novels such as *The Adventures of Huckleberry Finn*.

Readers took a fresh look at Dunbar's writing in the decades that followed. They came to understand that

Langston Hughes was the best-known poet of the Harlem
Renaissance of the 1920s.

Dunbar's home on North Summit Street in Dayton, Ohio, is now a museum maintained by the state of Ohio.

although he did write many dialect poems to meet public demand, he created loving portraits of his people in those verses. In his stories and magazine articles, readers discovered a sharp social critic who was unafraid to speak out about the unfair treatment of African Americans. They also found a champion of African-American achievement.

In 1903, in an essay titled "Representative American Negroes," Dunbar had written about accomplished men and women who represented black America in various lines of work. For example, he mentioned Booker T. Washington and W. E. B. Du Bois, two outstanding educators, and Will Marion Cook, the influential composer. He praised Mary Church Terrell for improving the lives of African-American women. He named the artist Henry Ossawa Tanner (1859–1937) and his father, Bishop Benjamin Tucker Tanner of the African Methodist Episcopal Church. And he mentioned a successful farmer, Junius G. Groves, the "potato king of Kansas," who had been born into slavery in 1859.[7]

All of these people, Dunbar said, shared certain qualities: "preparation, perseverance, bravery, patience, honesty and the power to seize the opportunity."[8] He could have been describing himself. Dunbar was hopeful that, in the near future, many more African Americans would contribute to American life. He wrote, "It is a little dark still, but there are warnings of the day and somewhere out of the darkness a bird is singing to the dawn."[9]

CHRONOLOGY

1872—Paul Laurence Dunbar is born in Dayton, Ohio, on June 27.

1876—Dunbar's parents, Joshua and Matilda Dunbar, divorce.

1878
−1891—Dunbar excels as a student in the Dayton public schools.

1888—*The Dayton Herald* prints three of Dunbar's poems.

1890—Dunbar publishes *The Tattler*, a newspaper for the African Americans of Dayton.

1891—Graduates from Central High School; works as an elevator operator at the Callahan Building in Dayton; writes stories and poems that begin to appear in magazines.

1892—Reads his poetry before a convention of the Western Association of Writers in Dayton; journalist James Newton Matthews writes a news article about Dunbar that is printed nationwide; Dunbar receives a letter of encouragement from Indiana poet James Whitcomb Riley; publishes his first book of poetry, *Oak and Ivy*.

1893—Attends the World's Columbian Exposition in Chicago, Illinois; meets the antislavery activist Frederick Douglass; befriends other notable young African Americans, including Mary Church Terrell, James Weldon Johnson, and Will Marion Cook.

1895—Works briefly for several newspapers, including the *Indianapolis World*; forms a friendship with Dr. Henry A. Tobey, an Ohio psychiatrist; begins corresponding with Alice Ruth Moore.

1896—Publishes a second volume of poetry, *Majors and Minors*, with Tobey's financial help; William Dean Howells favorably reviews *Majors and Minors*; Dodd, Mead and Company publishes *Lyrics of Lowly Life*.

1897—Meets Alice Moore for the first time; sails to England; writes the musical play *Dream Lovers* with Samuel Coleridge-Taylor; takes a job with the Library of Congress; settles in Washington, D.C.

1898—Marries Alice Moore in New York City; publishes *The Uncalled*, his first novel, and *Folks from Dixie*, a short-story collection.

1899—Publishes two books of poetry, *Lyrics of the Hearthside* and *Poems of Cabin and Field*; writes the musical show *Clorindy, the Origin of the Cakewalk* with Will Marion Cook; resigns from the Library of Congress; visits the Tuskegee Institute; develops pneumonia; travels to Denver, Colorado.

1900—Publishes *The Love of Landry*, a novel with a western setting, and *The Strength of Gideon and Other Stories*; returns to Washington, D.C., and learns that he has tuberculosis; is robbed during a racially motivated riot in New York City.

1901—Publishes a novel, *The Fanatics*; visits James Weldon Johnson in Florida; rides in President McKinley's inauguration parade; becomes increasingly dependent on alcohol.

1902—Publishes his last novel, *The Sport of the Gods*; writes *In Dahomey* with Cook; separates from Alice Dunbar; moves briefly to Chicago, then settles with his mother in Dayton.

1903—Publishes *Lyrics of Love and Laughter,* a book of poetry, and *In Old Plantation Days*, a story collection.

1904—Writes a presidential campaign poem for Theodore Roosevelt; publishes a book of short stories, *The Heart of Happy Hollow*.

1905—Rides in Roosevelt's inaugural parade; publishes a final volume of poetry, *Lyrics of Sunshine and Shadow*.

1906—Dies of tuberculosis on February 9.

WORKS BY PAUL LAURENCE DUNBAR

Poetry

Oak and Ivy, 1892
Majors and Minors, 1896
Lyrics of Lowly Life, 1896
Lyrics of the Hearthside, 1899
*Poems of Cabin and Field,** 1899
*Candle Lightin' Time,** 1901
Lyrics of Love and Laughter, 1903
*When Malindy Sings,** 1903
*Li'l' Gal,** 1904
Lyrics of Sunshine and Shadow, 1905
*Howdy, Honey, Howdy,** 1905
*Joggin' Erlong,** 1906

Novels

The Uncalled, 1898
The Love of Landry, 1900
The Fanatics, 1901
The Sport of the Gods, 1902

Short-Story Collections

Folks from Dixie, 1898
The Strength of Gideon and Other Stories, 1900
In Old Plantation Days, 1903
The Heart of Happy Hollow, 1904

*Illustrated collection of poems printed previously.

Works for the Stage

Dream Lovers, 1897. Music by Samuel Coleridge-Taylor.

Clorindy, or the Origin of the Cakewalk, 1898. Music by Will Marion Cook.

Uncle Eph's Christmas, 1899. Music by Will Marion Cook.

Jes Lak White Fo'ks, 1900. By Will Marion Cook with additional lyrics by Paul Laurence Dunbar.

In Dahomey, 1902. Music by Will Marion Cook; lyrics by Paul Laurence Dunbar and others.

CHAPTER NOTES

Chapter 1. A Worthy Singer

1. Edward F. Arnold, "Some Personal Reminiscences of Paul Laurence Dunbar," *Journal of Negro History*, October 1932, p. 401.

2. Ibid.

3. Paul Laurence Dunbar, "The Haunted Oak," in *Lyrics of Love and Laughter* (New York: Dodd, Mead and Company, 1903), p. 153.

4. Ibid., p. 156.

5. Arnold, p. 401.

6. Ibid.

7. W. S. Scarborough, "The Poet Laureate of the Negro Race," *A. M. E. Review*, October 1914, p. 140.

8. Arna Bontemps, "The Relevance of Paul Laurence Dunbar," in Jay Martin, ed., *A Singer in the Dawn: Reinterpretations of Paul Laurence Dunbar* (New York: Dodd, Mead and Company, 1975), p. 45.

9. James Weldon Johnson, *Along This Way* (New York: The Viking Press, 1933), pp. 159–160.

10. Michael L. La Blanc, ed., *Contemporary Black Biography: Profiles from the International Black Community* (Detroit: Gale Research, Inc., 1992), vol. 1, p. 37.

11. Nikki Giovanni, "Afterword," in Jay Martin, ed., *A Singer in the Dawn: Reinterpretations of Paul Laurence Dunbar*, p. 243.

12. Paul Laurence Dunbar, letter to Henry A. Tobey, July 13, 1895. Paul Laurence Dunbar Collection, series 1, box 1, Ohio Historical Society, Columbus.

Chapter 2. Being a Boy

1. Jean Wagner, *Black Poets of the United States from Paul Laurence Dunbar to Langston Hughes* (Urbana and Chicago: University of Illinois Press, 1973), p. 74.

2. Paul Laurence Dunbar, "Emancipation," Dayton, Ohio, *Herald*, 1890. Paul Laurence Dunbar Collection, series 4, box 10, Ohio Historical Society, Columbus.

3. Paul Laurence Dunbar, "A Boy's Summer Song," in *Lyrics of Sunshine and Shadow* (New York: Dodd, Mead and Company, 1905), p. 1.

4. Quoted in Michael W. Williams, ed., *The African American Encyclopedia* (New York: Marshall Cavendish, 1993), vol. 2, p. 400.

5. Paul Laurence Dunbar, "Our Martyred Soldiers," Dayton, Ohio, *Herald*, June 8, 1888. Paul Laurence Dunbar Collection, MSS 659, series 1, box 1, Ohio Historical Society.

6. Quoted in Jay Martin, "Paul Laurence Dunbar: Biography Through Letters," in Jay Martin, ed., *A Singer in the Dawn: Reinterpretations of Paul Laurence Dunbar* (New York: Dodd, Mead and Company, 1975), p. 22.

7. Ibid., p. 23.

8. Paul Laurence Dunbar, "Farewell Song." Program, Class of 1891, Commencement Exercises of Central High School at Grand Opera House, June 16, 1891. Paul Laurence Dunbar Collection, MSS 659, series 1, box 1, Ohio Historical Society, Columbus.

Chapter 3. Dreaming All the Time

1. Paul Laurence Dunbar, "One Man's Fortunes," in *The Strength of Gideon and Other Stories* (New York: Dodd, Mead and Company, 1900), p. 159.

2. James Whitcomb Riley, "The Old Swimmin'-Hole," in *"The Old Swimmin'-Hole" and Other Poems* (Indianapolis: The Bobbs-Merrill Company, 1912), p. 7.

3. Irwin Russell, "Mahsr John," in *Poems by Irwin Russell* (New York: The Century Company, 1888), p. 43.

4. Paul Laurence Dunbar, "The Ol' Tunes," in *Lyrics of Lowly Life* (New York: Dodd, Mead and Company, 1896), p. 122.

5. Paul Laurence Dunbar, "What's the Use of Dreaming." Paul Laurence Dunbar Collection, series 4, box 10, Ohio Historical Society, Columbus.

6. Quoted in Jay Martin, "Paul Laurence Dunbar: Biography Through Letters," in Jay Martin, ed., *A Singer in the Dawn: Reinterpretations of Paul Laurence Dunbar* (New York: Dodd, Mead and Company, 1975), p. 14.

7. Paul Laurence Dunbar, "Welcome Address to the Western Association of Writers," in *Oak and Ivy* (Dayton, Ohio: Press of the United Brethren Publishing House, 1892), p. 25.

8. Quoted in Martin, p. 14.

9. Ibid., p. 15.

10. Ibid.

11. Ibid.

12. Quoted in Virginia Cunningham, *Paul Laurence Dunbar and His Song* (New York: Dodd, Mead and Company, 1947), p. 74.

Chapter 4. Fame's Bright Sky

1. Paul Laurence Dunbar, dedication to *Oak and Ivy* (Dayton, Ohio. Press of the United Brethren Publishing House, 1892).

2. Paul Laurence Dunbar, "Ode to Ethiopia," in *Lyrics of Lowly Life* (New York: Dodd, Mead and Company, 1896), p. 31.

3. Paul Laurence Dunbar, "A Banjo Song," in *Lyrics of Lowly Life*, p. 42.

4. Paul Laurence Dunbar, letter to Matilda Dunbar, June 6, 1891. Paul Laurence Dunbar Collection, series 1, box 1, Ohio State Historical Society, Columbus.

5. Ibid.

6. Quoted in Dick Russell, *Black Genius and the American Experience* (New York: Carroll and Graf, 1998), p. 14.

7. Paul Laurence Dunbar, "The Colored Soldiers," in *Lyrics of Lowly Life*, p. 116.

8. Ibid., p. 117.

9. Paul Laurence Dunbar, "Frederick Douglass," in *The Complete Poems of Paul Laurence Dunbar* (New York: Dodd, Mead and Company, 1913), p. 6.

10. Ibid.

11. Ibid., p. 7.

12. Ibid.

13. Ibid.

14. Quoted in Linda Keck Wiggins, *The Life and Works of Paul Laurence Dunbar* (Naperville, Ill.: J. L. Nichols, 1907), p. 41.

15. Quoted in James B. Stronks, "Paul Laurence Dunbar and William Dean Howells," *The Ohio Historical Quarterly*, April 1958, pp. 97–98.

16. Ibid., p. 98.

17. Ibid.

Chapter 5. Pen and Voice

1. Paul Laurence Dunbar, "The Corn-Stalk Fiddle," in *Lyrics of Lowly Life* (New York: Dodd, Mead and Company, 1896), p. 35.

2. Quoted in Linda Keck Wiggins, *The Life and Works of Paul Laurence Dunbar* (Naperville, Ill.: J. L. Nichols, 1907), p. 66.

3. Paul Laurence Dunbar, "We Wear the Mask," in *Lyrics of Lowly Life*, p. 167.

4. William Dean Howells, "Introduction," in *Lyrics of Lowly Life*, p. xix.

5. Ibid.

6. Ibid.

7. Quoted in Pauline A. Young, "Paul Laurence Dunbar: An Intimate Glimpse," *Freedomways*, Fourth Quarter 1972, p. 320.

8. Ibid., p. 321.

9. Ibid.

10. Ibid., p. 325.

11. Ibid.

12. Quoted in James B. Stronks, "Paul Laurence Dunbar and William Dean Howells," *The Ohio Historical Quarterly*, April 1958, p. 105.

Chapter 6. The Caged Bird

1. Quoted in Kathryn Schneider Smith, ed., *Washington at Home* (Northridge, Calif.: Windsor Publications, 1988), p. 144.

2. Quoted in the Junior League of Washington, *The City of Washington* (New York: Alfred A. Knopf, 1977), p. 287.

3. Paul Laurence Dunbar, "Negro Society in Washington," *Saturday Evening Post*, December 14, 1901, p. 9.

4. Mary Church Terrell, *A Colored Woman in a White World* (Washington, D.C.: Ransdell, 1940), p. 111.

5. Paul Laurence Dunbar, "Little Brown Baby," in *Lyrics of the Hearthside* (New York: Dodd, Mead and Company, 1899), p. 139.

6. Ibid., p. 140.

7. Paul Laurence Dunbar, "Alexander Crummell— Dead," in *Lyrics of the Hearthside*, p. 76.

8. Ibid., p. 77.

9. Paul Laurence Dunbar, "Harriet Beecher Stowe," in *Lyrics of the Hearthside*, p. 97.

10. Alice M. Dunbar, "The Poet and His Song," in Alice Moore Dunbar-Nelson, *The Dunbar Speaker and Entertainer*

and The Poet and His Song (New York: G. K. Hall and Company, 1996), p. 325.

11. Ibid.

12. Quoted in Gossie Harold Hudson, "Paul Laurence Dunbar: The Regional Heritage of Dayton's First Black Poet," *Antioch Review*, Summer 1976, p. 435.

13. Quoted in Lerone Bennett, Jr., *Before the Mayflower: A History of Black America* (Chicago: Johnson Publishing, 1987), p. 276.

14. Paul Laurence Dunbar, "Recession Never," in *The Paul Laurence Dunbar Reader* (New York: Dodd, Mead and Company, 1975), p. 37.

15. Ibid.

16. Ibid., p. 39.

17. Alice M. Dunbar, p. 332.

18. Ibid.

19. Paul Laurence Dunbar, "Sympathy," in *Lyrics of the Hearthside*, pp. 40–41.

Chapter 7. An Unknown Country

1. Will Marion Cook, "Clorindy, the Origin of the Cakewalk," in Rosamond Gilder et al., eds., *Theatre Arts Anthology: A Record and a Prophecy* (New York: Theatre Arts Books, 1950), p. 227.

2. Ibid., p. 228.

3. Ibid., p. 232.

4. Quoted in W. E. B. Du Bois, *The Souls of Black Folk* (New York: Bantam Books, 1989), p. 31.

5. Quoted in Peter Revell, *Paul Laurence Dunbar* (Boston: Twayne Publishers, 1979), p. 49.

6. Gossie H. Hudson, "The Crowded Years: Paul Laurence Dunbar in History," in Jay Martin, ed., *A Singer in the Dawn: Reinterpretations of Paul Laurence Dunbar* (New York: Dodd, Mead and Company, 1975), p. 232.

7. Ibid., p. 235.

8. Du Bois, p. 39.

9. Paul Laurence Dunbar, *The Love of Landry* (New York: Dodd, Mead and Company, 1900), pp. 39–40.

10. Ibid., p. 40.

Chapter 8. No Rest

1. Paul Laurence Dunbar, *The Sport of the Gods*, in William L. Andrews, ed., *The African-American Novel in the Age of Reaction* (New York: Mentor, 1992), p. 586.

2. Gossie H. Hudson, "The Crowded Years: Paul Laurence Dunbar in History," in Jay Martin, ed., *A Singer in the Dawn: Reinterpretations of Paul Laurence Dunbar* (New York: Dodd, Mead and Company, 1975), p. 239.

3. James Weldon Johnson, *Along This Way* (New York: The Viking Press, 1933), p. 161.

4. Paul Laurence Dunbar, "The Poet," in *The Complete Poems of Paul Laurence Dunbar* (New York: Dodd, Mead and Company, 1913), p. 191.

5. Johnson, *Along This Way*, p. 161.

6. Ibid., p. 160.

7. Paul Laurence Dunbar, "Li'l' Gal," in *The Complete Poems of Paul Laurence Dunbar*, p. 207.

8. Quoted in Virginia Cunningham, *Paul Laurence Dunbar and His Song* (New York: Dodd, Mead and Company, 1947), p. 226.

Chapter 9. Back Home

1. James Weldon Johnson, *Along This Way* (New York: The Viking Press, 1933), p. 175.

2. Paul Laurence Dunbar, "Bein' Back Home," in *Lyrics of Sunshine and Shadow* (New York: Dodd, Mead and Company, 1905), p. 73.

3. Paul Laurence Dunbar, "Black Samson of Brandywine," in *The Complete Poems of Paul Laurence Dunbar* (New York: Dodd, Mead and Company, 1913), p. 206.

4. Paul Laurence Dunbar, "Dinah Kneading Dough," in *The Complete Poems of Paul Laurence Dunbar*, pp. 188–189.

5. Paul Laurence Dunbar, "Life's Tragedy," in *The Complete Poems of Paul Laurence Dunbar*, p. 225.

6. Paul Laurence Dunbar, *The Heart of Happy Hollow* (New York: Dodd, Mead and Company, 1904), p. v.

7. Paul Laurence Dunbar, "Compensation," in *Lyrics of Sunshine and Shadow* (New York: Dodd, Mead and Company, 1905), p. 61.

8. Mary Church Terrell, *A Colored Woman in a White World* (Washington, D.C.: Ransdell, 1940), p. 112.

9. Ibid.

10. Ibid.

11. Johnson, *Along This Way*, p. 161.

12. "Unpublished Letters of Paul Laurence Dunbar to a Friend," *The Crisis*, June 1920, p. 76.

13. Gossie H. Hudson, "The Crowded Years: Paul Laurence Dunbar in History," in Jay Martin, ed., *A Singer in the Dawn: Reinterpretations of Paul Laurence Dunbar* (New York: Dodd, Mead and Company, 1975), p. 238.

Chapter 10. Singing to the Dawn

1. Gossie H. Hudson, "The Crowded Years: Paul Laurence Dunbar in History," in Jay Martin, ed., *A Singer in the Dawn: Reinterpretations of Paul Laurence Dunbar* (New York: Dodd, Mead and Company, 1975), p. 238.

2. Quoted in Edward F. Arnold, "Some Personal Reminiscences of Paul Laurence Dunbar," *Journal of Negro History*, October 1932, p. 407.

3. Paul Laurence Dunbar, "A Death Song," in *The Complete Poems of Paul Laurence Dunbar* (New York: Dodd, Mead and Company, 1913), p. 142.

4. Quoted in Peter Revell, *Paul Laurence Dunbar* (Boston: Twayne Publishers, 1979), p. 166.

5. Allan Nevins, ed., *The Letters and Journal of Brand Whitlock* (New York: D. Appleton-Century Company, 1936), p. 50.

6. Ibid., p. 51.

7. Frank Lincoln Mather, ed., *Who's Who of the Colored Race* (Chicago: Frank Lincoln Mather, 1915), vol. 1, p. 125.

8. Paul Laurence Dunbar, "Representative American Negroes," in *The Paul Laurence Dunbar Reader* (New York: Dodd, Mead and Company, 1975), p. 59.

9. Ibid.

FURTHER READING

Christian, Charles M. *Black Saga: The African American Experience*. Boston: Houghton Mifflin, 1995.

Clinton, Catherine. *I, Too, Sing America: Three Centuries of African American Poetry*. Boston: Houghton Mifflin, 1998.

Dunbar, Paul Laurence. *The Collected Poetry of Paul Laurence Dunbar*, ed. Joanne M. Braxton. Charlottesville: University Press of Virginia, 1993.

———. *The Paul Laurence Dunbar Reader*, Jay Martin and Gossie H. Hudson., eds. New York: Dodd, Mead and Company, 1975.

Franklin, John Hope, and Alfred A. Moss, Jr. *From Slavery to Freedom* (Seventh Edition). New York: McGraw-Hill, Inc., 1994.

Gayle, Addison, Jr. *Oak and Ivy: A Biography of Paul Laurence Dunbar*. Garden City, N.Y.: Doubleday and Company, 1971.

Gentry, Tony. *Paul Laurence Dunbar*. New York: Chelsea House, 1989.

Hughes, Langston. *Famous American Negroes*. New York: Dodd, Mead and Company, 1954.

Martin, Jay, ed. *A Singer in the Dawn: Reinterpretations of Paul Laurence Dunbar*. New York: Dodd, Mead and Company, 1975.

McKissack, Pat. *Paul Laurence Dunbar: A Poet to Remember*. Chicago: Children's Press, 1984.

Revell, Peter. *Paul Laurence Dunbar*. Boston: Twayne Publishers, 1979.

Wagner, Jean. *Black Poets of the United States from Paul Laurence Dunbar to Langston Hughes*. Urbana and Chicago: University of Illinois Press, 1973.

INTERNET ADDRESSES

Wright State University Library
Contains Dunbar's poetry and William Dean Howells's introduction to *Lyrics of Lowly Life*, as well as sound recordings of some of Dunbar's poems.
<www.libraries.wright.edu/dunbar/>

University of Dayton
Includes information on the life of Paul Laurence Dunbar, photographs of Dunbar and his Dayton home, and sound recordings of selected poems.
<www.udayton.edu/~dunbar/>

INDEX

A

African-American life, 22–23, 50

Angelou, Maya, 12

"Aunt Mandy's Investment," 65

B

"A Banjo Song," 36

"Bein' Back Home," 95–97

Black Codes, 23

"Black Samson of Brandywine," 95, 97

Brooks, Gwendolyn, 12

Buffalo Soldiers, 68

Burns, Robert (Bud), 21, 95, 102

C

cakewalk, **74**

Campbell, James Edwin, 39

Carothers, James David, 39

Carver, George Washington, 79

Chicago, Illinois, 37, 95

Civil War, 16

Clorindy, the Origin of the Cakewalk, 76

Coleridge-Taylor, Samuel, 58, **59**

"The Colored Soldiers," 42

"Compensation," 100

Cook, Will Marion, 39, 42, 73–**77**, 93, 95, 109

"The Corn-Stalk Fiddle," 52

Crummell, Alexander, 19, 66

D

Davis, Varina Howell, 52–53

Dayton, Ohio, 15, 16, 18–19, **28**, 95

"A Death Song," 104

Denver, Colorado, 80, 82, 83

dialect poetry, 28–29, 31, 36, 54, 65, 104, 106

"Dinah Kneading Dough," 97–98

Dodd, Mead and Company, 53, 60, 83

Douglass, Frederick, 19, 39, 41–42, **43**, 44, 50

Douglass, Joseph, 42, **43**

Dream Lovers, 58

Du Bois, W. E. B., 79–80, 105, 109

Dunbar, Alice Ruth Moore (wife), 55, 56, **57**, 60, 63, 66–67, 75, 76–78, 80, 86, 91, 92, 95, 105

Dunbar, Joshua (father), 16–18

Dunbar, Matilda (mother), **14**, 15–17, 17, 18, 105

Dunbar, Paul Laurence, **9, 70, 96, 101**

   alcoholism, 85–86

   courtship and marriage, 55–56, 63

   death and burial, 102, 103–104

   early life, 15–18

   employment, 27, 37, 39, 44, 61, 71, 78

   essays, 69, 71, 108–109

experiences in England,
  56–60
fiction, 8, 26–27, 60, 64, 65,
  82–82, 86, 98, 99
high school, 19–21, **20,**
  23–24
honored by Atlanta
  University, 78
illness, 75, 80, 83, 86, 91,
  93, 95
literary aims, 55, 66-67, 90
poetry, 11, 12–13, 17, 21,
  31, 33, 34, 35–36, 39, 42,
  44–45, 52, 53–54, 65, 66,
  71–72, 88–90, 95–98,
  100, 104
reading habits, 27–29, 31
recitals, 11, 42, 52, 58,
  85–86
regrets, 98, 100, 101
rejection of Booker T.
  Washington's philosophy,
  79
robbed of money, 84
separation from wife, 92, 95
social life, 64
theatrical work, 58, 74–76,
  93
writing habits, 10–11, 75,
  90
Dunbar, Robert (Rob), 17, 18,
  95
Dunbar, William (Buddy), 17,
  18

E
"Emancipation," 17

F
The Fanatics, 86

Field, Eugene, 28
Folks From Dixie, 8, 65
"Frederick Douglass," 44–45

G
Giovanni, Nikki, 12

H
Hammon, Jupiter, 54
Harlem Renaissance, 105–106
Harper, Frances Ellen Watkins,
  54–55
"The Haunted Oak," 10–11
The Heart of Happy Hollow, 98
Hogan, Ernest, 76, 83
Howells, William Dean, 46, **47,**
  50, 54, 66
Hughes, Langston, 12, 106,
  107

I
In Dahomey, 93

J
"Jimsella," 65
Johnson, J. Rosamond, 90–91
Johnson, James Weldon, 40,
  88, **89,** 90, 95, 101, 106

L
LeDroit Park, 61, **62,** 63
"Life's Tragedy," 98
"Li'l' Gal," 91
"Little Brown Baby," 65
The Love of Landry, 82
lynching. *See* racial violence
"The Lynching of Jube
  Benson," 99
Lyrics of Love and Laughter,
  97–98
Lyrics of Lowly Life, 53–54

Lyrics of Sunshine and Shadow, 100
Lyrics of the Hearthside, 65

M

Majors and Minors, 45–46, 48
Matthews, James Newton, 33–34
McKay, Claude, 106
McKinley, William, 46, 88, 92
minstrel shows, 75

N

New York City, 49–50, **51**, 80, 93

O

Oak and Ivy, 35–36, 39, 45
"Ode to Ethiopia," 35–36, 39
"The Ol' Tunes," 31, 34, 39
"An Old-Time Christmas," 82–83
"One Man's Fortunes," 26–27
"Our Martyred Soldiers," 21

P

pan-Africanism, 19, 66
plantation poetry, 29–30
Poems of Cabin and Field, 65
"The Poet," 88, 90
Pond, James, Major, 50

R

racial violence, 8, 10, 68–69, 83–84, 99–100
"Representative American Negroes," 108-109
Riley, James Whitcomb, 28–**29**, 34
Roosevelt, Theodore, 68, 80, 92
Russell, Irwin, 30, 106

S

segregation, 41, 63
slavery, 15–16
Spanish-American War, 67–68
The Sport of the Gods, 87
Stowe, Harriet Beecher, 66
The Strength of Gideon and Other Stories, 82
"Sympathy," 71–72

T

Tattler, 22–23
Tennyson, Alfred, Lord, 27
Terrell, Mary Church, 39, 64, 100, 104, 109
Tobey, Henry A., 45, 103–104
Tuskegee Institute, 50-51, 78–79, **81**
Twain, Mark, 50, 106

U

The Uncalled, 60, 64–65
Uncle Eph's Christmas, 76
Uncle Tom's Cabin, 66
Underground Railroad, 16

W

Washington, Booker T., 50, 78–79, 109
Washington, D.C., 61–63, 83
"We Wear the Mask," 53
Wells, Ida B., 39
Western Association of Writers, 32–33, 36
Wheatley, Phyllis, 54
Whitlock, Brand, 104
Williams, Bert, **94**
World's Columbian Exposition, 37, **38**, 40–41
Wright, Orville, 21–22
Wright, Richard, 106